Student's Vegetarian Cookbook

Student's Vegetarian Cookbook

Quick, Easy, Cheap,
and Tasty Vegetarian Recipes

Carole Raymond

REVISED

THREE RIVERS PRESS • NEW YORK

Published by Three Rivers Press, New York, New York.
Member of the Crown Publishing Group, a division of Random House, Inc.
www.randomhouse.com

THREE RIVERS PRESS and the Tugboat design are registered trademarks of Random House, Inc.

A previous edition of this work was published by Prima Publishing in 1997.

Printed in the United States of America

The information for pages xxiii and xxiv was compiled by EarthSave International. Used by permission.

Library of Congress Cataloging-in-Publication Data
Raymond, Carole
   Student's vegetarian cookbook : quick, easy, cheap, and tasty vegetarian recipes / Carole Raymond.
      p.   cm.
   Includes index.
      1. Vegetarian cookery. 2. Quick and easy cookery. 3. Low budget cookery. I. Title.
TX837.R3793 2003
641.5'636—dc21   2003006863

ISBN 0-7615-1170-9
10 9 8

Second Edition

To my mother, Rose, and stepfather,
Henry, and to Yoda and Lucky

Contents

7. Fast Foods, Vegetarian-Style: Sandwiches, Tortilla Wraps, Sushi Rolls, and Pizzas   89

8. Bean Meals 133

9. Grain Meals   153

10. Noodles   171

Preface

Welcome to vegetarian cooking. There has never been a better time to appreciate the sights, smells, flavors, and textures of a meatless diet.

More and more people are recognizing how vegetarian cooking will benefit their health and please their palates. As markets fill with broader arrays of wholesome foods, even the student or first-time cook can easily turn a basketful of vegetables, grains, and other simple ingredients into delicious, quick, and inexpensive meals. Consider some of the bonuses of vegetarian eating:

- Eating vegetarian means that you can make a great meal with all the necessary nutrients and no meat in just one entree. Pasta, pizza, tacos, quesadillas, fajitas, stir-fries, simple one-pot soups, salads, creamy polenta with sautéed vegetables, a bowl of chili, or a baked potato topped with steaming vegetables; all these foods can easily fill the center of any plate.

- For the health-conscious, vegetarianism will help you look and feel great. Vegetarian meals are lower in fat than meals that revolve around meat, and this may explain why vegetarians are on the average trimmer than their meat-eating counterparts. Eating lots of vegetables is appealing because it helps combat the "Freshman 15," the mythical number of pounds a first-year college student is expected to gain eating high-calorie fast food.

- If you like to eat, but don't like cleaning up, vegetarian cooking has another bonus. Without the animal fat that sticks to pans and plates when you cook meat, cleanup is a snap.

- Cultures all over the world center their cuisine on plant foods. As you dip into vegetarian cooking, your plate will fill with the accumulated flavors of many culinary traditions.

If you are just starting out, you may need a helping hand over a few small hurdles. *The Animal Rights Handbook* estimates that the average American will eat 1 calf, 3 lambs, 11 cows, 23 hogs, 45 turkeys, and 1,097 chickens in a lifetime. You probably grew up thinking of meat as the virtual pillar of the American way of life. The government promoted it, your third-grade teacher placed steaks and drumsticks squarely in the middle of the food chart, and television told us meat would make us "real people."

The dominant meat-eating culture is often ignorant about and consequently maligns vegetarians. Here are some of the myths commonly associated with vegetarianism and the facts that dispel them.

- *Vegetarians are weak and frail.* Some of the planet's largest and strongest animals live by eating vegetables—after all, elephants, bulls, gorillas, and stallions are all vegetarians. There are many renowned vegetarian athletes, including Dave Scott, one of the greatest triathletes in the world.

- *Vegetarians do not get enough protein.* You can get all the protein you need just by eating a variety of foods every day. The average American diet far exceeds healthy protein requirements.

- *Vegetarians are a tired lot.* If you are looking for more energy, you will get it from eating complex carbohydrates like whole grain pasta and whole grain bread, not from meat.

- *Humans are naturally carnivores.* Human beings are primates whose teeth, intestinal structure, and dietary needs are ideal for eating plant foods, not flesh. (Many believe that eating meat began during the Ice Age when plant food became scarce.)

- *Health professionals find vegetarian eating a questionable choice.* The Physicians' Committee for Responsible Medicine recently called for four new food groups (whole grains, vegetables, fruits, and legumes) and lists dairy products and meat as optional.

Calcium and Vegetarianism

Calcium is an important nutrient for building strong bones that will last a lifetime. Vegetarians get their calcium from the same place cows do, from green things that grow in the ground and from calcium-fortified food. Milk and cheese are also excellent sources of calcium, but the definitive word about how much you need isn't in yet, so in the meantime, it makes sense to be moderate in the amount you choose. Here is a list of calcium sources to help guide your choices.

Excellent Sources of Calcium

Bok choy
Calcium-fortified orange juice
Calcium-fortified tofu (processed with calcium sulfate)
Calcium-fortified soy milk
Calcium-fortified rice milk
Calcium-fortified breakfast cereal and snack bars
Collard greens
Firm cheese: cheddar, Parmesan, Jack, part-skim
    mozzarella, Swiss
Kale
Nonfat dairy milk
Nonfat yogurt

Good Sources of Calcium

Black beans
Broccoli
Corn tortillas

Dried figs
Navy beans
Sesame seeds
Tahini (sesame butter)

Minor Sources of Calcium

Butternut squash
Carrots
Lentils
Oranges
Sweet potato

Building a healthy skeleton requires more than only calcium. Bones, like muscles, respond to use. When you exercise, they become stronger. Vitamin D is also part of the story. It is essential to help you absorb calcium, and you can get it from your diet and the sun, which triggers cells in the skin to manufacture the vitamin. So when you're outside jogging or walking, you're building strong bones, too.

Fast-Forward

Learning your way out of a meat-eating culture, especially as a beginning cook, can appear daunting. Luckily, attitudes are changing. Many people now recognize that a meat-based diet paves the road to many forms of illness, for both humans and the environment. A well-balanced vegetarian diet can provide all the nutrients we need. Many people quickly discover that vegetarian meals surpass their taste expectations.

No matter how much you love to eat, there are times when you don't feel like squarely facing the stove. Here's a list of 10 quick meals that set aside the sauté pan and instead rely on a can opener, commercial grocery options, and frozen vegetables.

Top 10 List of No-Time-to-Cook Meals

1. Celebrate Soup—Turn a simple cup or can of soup into a filling meal. Add some extras: cooked pasta, rice, beans, or frozen vegetables.

2. Hearty Green Salad—Start with a bag of commercially prepared, prewashed salad greens. On a bed of greens, add slices of tomato and carrots. Sprinkle with canned kidney beans, sunflower seeds, or grated cheese. Drizzle with dressing.

3. Pasta and Sauce—Boil up a pot of noodles. Open a jar of pasta sauce; heat it in a saucepan with a handful of frozen mixed vegetables. Pour the sauce mixture over the noodles and sprinkle with Parmesan cheese.

4. Chili on Toast—Heat 3/4 cup commercial vegetarian chili with a handful of frozen corn. Toast a slice of whole grain bread. Spoon hot chili over the toast, and top with optional extras: grated cheese or yogurt, salsa, green onions, chopped cilantro.

5. Tacos—Fill a warm corn tortilla with creamy refried beans, lettuce, tomato, salsa, and a sprinkle of grated Cheddar cheese. Fold and eat.

6. Popular Pizza—Make a gourmet pizza in minutes. Spread a ready-made frozen pizza shell or seasoned Boboli with prepared pizza sauce. Drain the liquid from a jar of marinated artichoke hearts. Top the sauce with the artichokes, thin onion slices, olives, bell pepper rings, and tomato slices. Scatter cheese on top, and bake according to pizza crust directions.

7. Hot Baked Potatoes—Pick your favorite or try all four:
   - Taco Potato: Top a potato with warm canned black beans, salsa, and grated cheese.
   - Sauced Potato: Open the potato wide and mash the inside with a fork. Pour on 1/2 cup warm commercial veggie soup (such as split pea, lentil, or minestrone).

- Veggie Potato: Top the potato with a mixture of steamed frozen vegetables, a squeeze of lemon juice, salt, and pepper.
- Sweet Potato: Mix 1/2 cup of plain yogurt with a teaspoon of tahini, and spoon it over a baked or steamed sweet potato; sprinkle with chopped green onions, and add a side of seasoned rice.

8. Virtual Burgers and Hot Dogs—Veggie burgers and tofu dogs (available in most commercial supermarkets) are a quick fix. Neither has the taste nor texture of their meat counterparts, so if that's what you expect, get ready for something different. Layer a bun or piece of bread with fresh lettuce, tomatoes, and sliced onion. Add the burger or tofu dog and top with your favorite condiments.

9. Tangy Yogurt—Add a handful of granola and sliced fruit to an 8-ounce container of yogurt. Stir and eat.

10. Whipped Drinks—In a blender, whip up a meal with soy milk and fresh fruit. Ripe bananas and berries make a good beginning.

When you are ready for more food adventures, the *Student's Vegetarian Cookbook* will give you the tools you need to bring a world of fresh and varied tastes onto your table. Grab a cutting board and follow these recipes to good health and great eating!

Acknowledgments

Thank you to Richard, Camela, and Jonathan; and to my friends, Toni Barrientos, Phyllis Beals, Anna Beck, Nancy Byles, Roberta Gross, Lee Johnson, and Patti Walther. Special thanks to Roberta Miller.

Special thanks also to my editors, Denise Sternad and Marjorie Lery, and everyone else at Prima and Three Rivers Press who helped make this book a reality.

Introduction
"It Bugs Me"

Celebrated author Andrei Codrescu, whose keen observations of American culture can be heard regularly on National Public Radio, has this to say in his book *Zombification: Stories from National Public Radio* (St. Martin's Press) about how eating meat affects the planet, animals, and your health and why building yet another Burger King bugs him.

> *Number one, they kill cows; number two, the cows they kill graze on the sites of murdered forests; number three, the cows they kill that killed the forests are full of hormones; number four, the hormone-filled cows they kill that killed the forests are full of bad-for-your-heart fat; number five, the bad-for-your-heart-hormone-filled-forest-killing-dead-cows are wrapped in bad-for-the-earth-plastic.*

What is a Whopper or Big Mac worth, and are you willing to pay the price? Here are facts from EarthSave International about eating meat that may disturb you:

- Livestock consume 70 percent of U.S. grain production. Twenty million people die each year as a result of malnutrition and starvation. Americans could feed 100,000,000 people by reducing their intake of meat by just 10 percent.

- One acre of prime land can produce many pounds of edible product. Here are a few examples:
  30,000 pounds of apples
  40,000 pounds of potatoes
  50,000 pounds of tomatoes
  250 pounds of beef

- Livestock—cattle, poultry, goats, sheep—totaling 15 billion worldwide now outnumber people three to one. Livestock graze on half of the world's land mass. The explosion of livestock populations has resulted in a parallel explosion of animal wastes that pollute surface and ground water. U.S. livestock produce 230,000 pounds of excrement per second. The amount of waste created by a 10,000-head feed lot is equal to the waste of a city of 110,000 people.

- World livestock production is now a significant factor in the emission of two of the four global warming gasses: carbon dioxide and methane. Every steak we eat has the same effect as a 25-mile drive in a typical American car.

- Each year, an estimated 125,000 square miles of rainforest are permanently destroyed, bringing about the extinction of approximately 1,000 plant and animal species.

- Producing 1 pound of feedlot steak results in the loss of 35 pounds of topsoil. It takes 200 to 1,000 years to form 1 inch of topsoil.

- It takes 2,500 gallons of water to produce 1 edible pound of beef. It takes 49 gallons of water to produce 1 edible pound of apples.

- Eighty percent of the meat produced in the United States contains drugs that are passed on to you when you eat it.

- Animal products contain large quantities of saturated fat and cholesterol and have no dietary fiber. The U.S. Surgeon General has stated that 68 percent of all diseases are diet related. A diet rich in fruits, vegetables, and grains (and free from animal products) can prevent, improve, and sometimes cure breast cancer, osteoporosis, prostate cancer, impotence, and obesity.

- Seventy-five percent of federal poultry inspectors say they would not eat chicken.

Organic Food

One of the greatest changes in grocery stores in recent years has been the popularity of organic food. It is expensive, but as the demand continues to increase, organic products will become more affordable. In the fall of 2002, the United States Department of Agriculture's (USDA's) rules for the production and labeling of organic food became effective. The regulations prohibit the use of genetic engineering, irradiation, and sewage sludge in certified organic production and handling of food. In general, the use of all synthetic substances, along with petroleum-based fertilizers, is prohibited, and organic food cannot be mixed with nonorganic varieties in stores.

The Genetically Modified Organisms (GMO) Controversy

The current revolution of biotechnology in food production is at the center of one of the planet's most important debates. Technology now enables food producers to go beyond the natural boundaries of nature by transferring genes from one species to another species. For example, moth or fish genes can be engineered into plants to make them more pesticide resistant. Many people feel we need to evaluate this new technology before we proceed further. The United States still does not require labeling of genetically engineered foods; however in Europe, the European Union has strict regulations that refuse to accept GMO crops from the United States. Change is on the way in this country. Recently, Oregon introduced a ballot measure requiring labeling, but so far voters have rejected the proposal.

What Can You Do?

Each individual has the opportunity to make a difference in creating a sustainable world for ourselves and future generations.

There is no way to escape the ecological cost of the choices we make, but there are ways to cut the price.

One of the significant choices you can make is to eat a vegetarian diet. This cookbook will teach you how to select and prepare fresh produce and other staples for vegetarian eating. The recipes collected here will help you to cook simple everyday meals to add to your list of lifelong favorites.

CHAPTER 1

Shop Smart—
Cook Smarter

Having food in the kitchen is 90 percent of the cooking battle, so begin your vegetarian adventure with a trip to the supermarket. Check out natural food stores and ethnic groceries. Look for supermarkets and neighborhood co-ops that sell items from bins where you scoop out what you need. Without the excess packaging on the product, you save a lot of money and there is less to recycle. Farmer's markets are a great place to find cheap, often organically grown, fresh fruits and vegetables.

When you buy fresh fruits and vegetables, buy them in small quantities. That way you won't find yourself staring at rotting produce in the refrigerator, and if you shop more than once a week, you'll find it easier to buy food that suits your mood.

As you roll your cart down the supermarket aisles, you'll see that the layout is anything but accidental. Some displays are set up to create a mini–traffic jam, so everyone pauses long enough to add more items to their carts. Look out for "endcap" displays designed to encourage impulse shopping. Market researchers have found that when background music slows from 108 beats per minute to 60 beats per minute, supermarket sales increase by 40 percent. Do most of your shopping at the perimeter of the store where you'll find the freshest, most healthful foods. Enjoy the tunes, eat the free food samples, and shop with your own plan in mind.

Compare the price of the store labels with the same brand-name item. Store labels are usually cheaper and comparable or better in quality. Big food manufacturers pay supermarkets enormous slotting fees to gain shelf space, and brand-name advertising budgets can reach over $100 million for a single product. As the consumer, you absorb the cost. Larger-sized packages are usually, but not always, cheaper. Two 14-ounce cans of tomatoes may be cheaper than one 28-ounce can. Handwritten signs along the aisles often make shoppers think a product is on sale when it may not be. Get to know the price of the foods you buy so you will know a bargain when you see it.

Check the expiration dates on perishable foods like dairy products, cereals, and bread. The freshest product is usually in the back of the display, and a handwritten sign by a perishable item may be a way to get you to buy a product that is about to expire.

In the cereal aisle, the ready-to-eat, whole grain cereals are usually on the bottom shelf, while the overprocessed, sugar-laden cereals are lined up at eye level. Read the labels and look for whole grain cereals like Shredded Wheat and Grape-Nuts. Buying cereal grains like old-fashioned rolled oats and cooking them yourself will save you money, and they make hearty meals.

When you arrive at the checkout stand with a basketful of fresh vegetarian food, it may surprise you to find that your grocery bill is less than you expected. Dollar for dollar, you get a lot more grains, beans, fruits, and vegetables than you do meat.

A Guide for Picking and Keeping Some of the Best Stuff at the Market

The market can be an overwhelming place to a new vegetarian. How do you know you are getting the freshest produce? What does a parsnip look like? And where is the tofu? Here is a guide that will help you overcome any anxiety you may have about selecting and storing fresh, ripe fruits, vegetables, soy foods, and whole grains.

Fresh Produce

Buy fruits and vegetables individually rather than in pre-packaged sacks or containers—that way you avoid wilted and bruised produce. Even if they are a bargain, chances are you will end up discarding some. When you get home, remove fruit from plastic bags, because plastic holds moisture and causes fruit to mold. Unlike fruit, most vegetables last longest tightly wrapped in plastic. Produce keeps best refrigerated. Store vegetables in their own crisper. If they are sitting with fruit, the ethylene gas from the fruit can cause premature brown spotting on vegetables. Do not wash fruits, particularly berries, before storing, because it hastens their deterioration. Wash fruit immediately before serving.

Apples If you find apples on sale, but the color is less than perfect, the quality of the fruit is probably still good inside. Avoid any that are soft or have bruised spots. Refrigerated apples will keep for 2 weeks or more.

Artichokes Choose an artichoke that feels heavy for its size and has compact, fresh-looking leaves. Dark outer leaves sometimes indicate cold-weather damage. Don't let that stop you from buying it. Eating an artichoke is a unique experience (See "Deconstructed Artichoke" on page 190).

Arugula   This calcium-rich green grows almost any time of the year. The mature leaves add piquancy to salads and soups. Arugula will keep for a few days in the refrigerator.

Asparagus   Look for tightly closed, compact tips, and firm brittle stalks. They are best eaten as soon as possible. Before cooking, snap off the tough lower stem ends and discard them. Rinse stalks under gently running water to remove any sand.

Avocados   You know an avocado is ripe when it yields very slightly to the pressure of your thumb. If you bring home one that's not quite ready for eating, you can hasten the ripening process by putting the avocado in a paper bag with a banana, at room temperature. Once ripe, avocados spoil quickly. A ready-to-eat avocado will keep in prime condition in the refrigerator for 4 to 7 days. To prepare an avocado, slice it in half lengthwise. Remove the seed. Cut lengthwise and crosswise slices in the flesh, making a grid. Scoop the avocado cubes out of the shells with a spoon.

Bananas   When buying bananas, buy some that are ripe, some not quite ripe, and a few green ones. That way they will be ready when you are. After a banana is ripe (but never before), put it in the refrigerator. (Once chilled, they won't sweeten.) Don't worry if the skin darkens after refrigeration. The fruit will still be good inside. A banana is in prime eating condition when it is dotted with brown "sugar" flecks.

Beans   Green beans can be yellow or green depending on their variety. Their color should be bright, and they should snap easily and have a velvety feel. They will keep for about 5 days, refrigerated. Steam or stir-fry them until they are crisp-tender, and serve seasoned with salt and pepper and a splash of lemon juice.

Beets   Beet roots should be smooth and firm. They will keep for about 2 weeks in the refrigerator. Peel and then shred or grate raw beets and toss them into salads. If preparing cooked beets, trim the leaf stem to about 1 inch, and boil or steam them with their skins on until tender. Lightly squeeze the beets when they are cool, and they will easily slip out of their jackets.

Broccoli   For the best flavor, choose broccoli with dark green florets and tiny buds. Yellowing florets and large thick stems are signs that broccoli is past its prime. Broccoli is delicious lightly steamed, sautéed, used in stir-fries, and even eaten raw.

Brussels Sprouts   Look for small, firm, compact heads with bright green color. Avoid large puffy ones or heads with dark spots or insect damage. Overcooking results in mushy, bitter-tasting vegetables. These minicabbages are tastiest when lightly steamed for 5 to 7 minutes. Cut off the stem end before steaming. Serve with a squeeze of lemon juice, and season with salt and pepper.

Cabbage   Green and red cabbage have survived since prehistoric times. They are versatile, cheap, and will surprise you with how much flavor they add to vegetarian meals. Select a small, bright-colored, firm head that feels heavy for its size. Cabbage will keep for more than 2 weeks, refrigerated.

Cabbage, Chinese   This is a generic name for a variety of greens used in Asian cooking. Two of the most popular are bok choy and celery cabbage. Look for bok choy with dark green leaves and thick white stems. Celery cabbage should be uniformly light green. The entire vegetable is usable. Chinese and celery cabbage are good in stir-fries and soups, or eat them steamed or sautéed as a side dish.

Cantaloupe   In selecting a cantaloupe, be sure its exterior is covered with a creamy-colored netting. A large smooth spot is a bad sign, and the stem end should be smooth without rough fibers showing. Most important, it should have a sweet aroma. Wrap cut melons in plastic, and do not remove the seeds until you are ready to eat the melon, since the seeds keep the melon moist.

Carrots   Look for carrots that are firm, not flabby. If the carrot is large and has a thick neck, the lighter-colored core will be large and thick too. For eating purposes, the core should be small because the good taste comes from the deep orange outside that stores the sugar. Carrots do not need peeling.

Cauliflower   Buy compact white heads free of speckles and smudges. Eat cauliflower raw or cooked. It keeps for about a week, refrigerated.

Chiles   Look for chiles with smooth, tight skins. Refrigerated in a plastic bag, fresh chiles will keep for about 5 days. The heat of a chile is in the ribs and seeds that are inside, and the heat can vary widely among the different kinds. Cut the chile open like a book; if you want to turn down the heat, remove ribs and seeds. Avoid touching your eyes or face while handling chiles.

Corn   Fresh sweet corn is a summer crop that holds up well when frozen, so enjoy it year-round. Buy frozen corn in bags, because then it is easy to scoop out just what you need.

Cucumbers   When selecting cucumbers, make sure you know what *not* to buy. Overmature cucumbers have a puffy, dull appearance. The skin of most supermarket cucumbers is coated with wax, so peel them before eating. Eat cucumbers raw.

Eggplants   Choose eggplants that are firm and have shiny, dark skin. The cap should look fresh and green. Never eat eggplant raw—it contains a toxin called solanine. Cooking eliminates the danger. Once cooked, you can eat the skin too. Eggplants submit to almost any cooking technique.

Garlic   Look for good-sized garlic with plump cloves free of soft spots. It is easier and faster to peel one or two big cloves than six tiny ones. Unpeeled garlic will stay fresh for weeks. Store garlic in a cool, dry place, but not in the refrigerator. Refrigerate jars of prepared garlic packed in oil. To prepare fresh garlic, first remove a clove from the bulb. Peel the clove by putting it on a cutting board and gently smashing it with the side of a large knife. The skin will slip off, and the flattened garlic will be easy to use. If you need small pieces, chop or mince by rocking your knife blade across the garlic. Hold down the front of the knife with the palm of your hand and cut, repeatedly pushing the garlic pieces back into a heap as you go.

Ginger   Do not let these knobby-looking roots scare you. Ginger is a fragrant addition to many vegetarian meals. Covered with plastic wrap, it will keep refrigerated for 2 weeks. You can also freeze ginger and grate it frozen. If the roots are large, you do not have to buy the whole thing; just break off an inch or two. Thin-skinned gingerroot needs no peeling. The strongest flavor is just beneath the skin.

Grapefruit   Choose grapefruits that are firm, spring to the touch, and feel heavy for their size. A heavy grapefruit indicates that it is full of juice. Grapefruit keeps for up to 8 weeks, refrigerated.

Grapes   Good grapes have a velvety, powdery appearance. Too much handling will give grapes a smooth and shiny look. If the stems look dry and brown, they are past their peak flavor.

Greens (collards, kale, chard, mustard)   Collards and kale are both members of the cabbage family. They look tough and leathery, but once cooked, they become almost silky and soft. Chard is a member of the beet family. To prepare greens, first discard any yellow or damaged leaves. Strip the leaves from large or tough stems and discard the stems. To cut the leaves, stack, bundle, or crumple them together with one hand while you slice with the other hand. Use greens in soups and stir-fries, or steamed as a yummy side dish drizzled with olive oil and a squeeze of lemon. Mustard greens are good in stir-fries and salads, and their peppery taste adds spark to a sandwich. Look for bundles with small, young leaves.

Kiwi   This fruit softens at room temperature and is ready to eat when it yields slightly to the touch. Eat kiwis peeled or unpeeled. After washing the kiwi, you'll barely notice the peel on thin slices. Scoop kiwis from the half shell, or eat them like apples, skin and all. (The skin is slightly tart.) Store ripened kiwis in the refrigerator. They will last up to 3 weeks. One fuzzy, lime-shaped, green fruit offers 125 percent of the vitamin C you need each day.

Leeks   Leeks are a member of the onion family but less pungent in taste. They resemble giant scallions and are good for soups and marinated vegetable plates. Use only the white and light green part near the bulb. Rinse well under running water to remove the sand and gravel that collect in their overlapping leaves. They are sold in bunches of three or four, or you can buy just one.

Lemons and Limes   The best lemons and limes have a fine-textured skin and are heavy for their size. Avoid fruit that is soft or spongy feeling. Look at the stem; that's where signs of aging begin. Get more juice from the fuit by gently rolling it on the counter and applying pressure with your hand before you cut it. This helps break the interior cells of the fruit. If you don't have a lemon squeezer, insert a fork into the center of a cut lemon or lime and twist to juice.

Lettuce   Lettuce is about the only produce that has managed to avoid becoming a processed food. You will not find it canned, frozen, or dehydrated. Forget iceberg lettuce, those tight round heads that look like green bowling balls. (It costs less and keeps longer than other kinds of lettuce, but it's the least nutritious and according to some, the least flavorful.) Pick dark green romaine, Boston, Bibb, or loose-leaf lettuces (redleaf and greenleaf).

Mushrooms   There are many varieties of mushrooms, but creminis or Italian mushrooms are the ones you are sure to see in most markets. Choose mushrooms with closed caps; when they open and look like umbrellas, it is a sign they have been hanging around the store too long. Store mushrooms in a paper bag in the refrigerator, never in plastic; they will keep for several days. Just before using fresh mushrooms, wipe them with a paper towel. Don't wash them because they'll become waterlogged and have less flavor when cooked.

Onions   The most common onions used for cooking are white or yellow. Sweet onions, like Bermudas, are good raw in salads and sandwiches. Choose onions that have their protective skin, are symmetrical, and are heavy for their size. Avoid those with soft or discolored spots and "sprouters"; they are old. Store onions in a cool, dry place, and always keep a few on hand. If you only need half an onion, chop the whole thing, and store what's left in the refrigerator. It will keep for several days, and you'll have a head start on tomorrow's meal. If chopping an onion causes your eyes to water, chilling the onion in the refrigerator for a few minutes will help ease the problem. Onions contain a substance called sulfur oxide. When it comes in contact with the moisture in your eyes, it forms a compound similar to sulfuric acid. That's why your eyes burn.

Oranges Do not depend on color to determine whether an orange is ripe and ready to eat. Instead, look for oranges that are firm and feel heavy for their size; this indicates lots of juice. Store them in the refrigerator for up to 6 weeks.

Parsnips Most people grow up without tasting parsnips. Try one if you are feeling adventurous. Parsnips look like an off-white carrot and have a unique nutlike flavor and a mild fragrance. Look for smooth, firm, well-shaped roots that are small to medium in size; large ones are likely to have woody cores, which must be removed. Peel them before using. They add sweetness to stews and soups and are tasty steamed, sautéed, or baked. They will keep for several weeks in the refrigerator.

Pears Growers pick pears before they are ripe, and they wind up in the produce department rock hard and bitter tasting. To achieve the sweet, buttery flavor that makes pears so delicious, ripen them in a warm place for 2 to 3 days or longer. Putting them in a perforated paper bag hastens the ripening process. They are ready to eat when the flesh around the stem yields to gentle pressure.

Peas, Garden, and Chinese Snow Peas Most peas sold in markets are frozen. They are one of the few vegetables that hold their taste when processed. Chinese snow peas are tiny inside, and the pod is tender, so they are eaten whole. One of the best ways to enjoy fresh peas is to eat them raw. Use fresh peas as soon as possible.

Peppers, Bell   Red, green, or yellow—they are all good. The green ones are usually the cheapest, and you can often use them interchangeably. However, for roasted red peppers, there is no substitution.

Potatoes   Russet potatoes have a brown skin and are good for baking. White and red potatoes are good for all-around use: boiling, frying, mashing, and roasting. Watch out for potatoes with a greenish cast; they will taste bitter. Buy a few at a time if you are cooking for one person, and store them in a cool, dry place. It does not take long for a big bag of potatoes to start sprouting and grow moldy. Pare off potato eyes, green spots, and blemishes before using. You don't need to peel potatoes.

Radishes   Buy firm, bright-looking radishes with green, crisp leaves and smooth, firm roots.

Spinach   If you buy spinach by the bunch, float the leaves in a big pot or bowl of water. The sand that clings to the leaves will sink to the bottom.

Sprouts, Mung Bean   The freshest sprouts are pearl-white and have not started to turn yellow. Store them for only 1 or 2 days in a sealed plastic bag in the refrigerator. Use them in stir-fries.

Squash, Summer   Zucchini is the best known, and it's available year-round. Choose squash that are small for their size, crisp, and free of wrinkled skin. They will keep refrigerated for a week.

Squash, Winter   Look for hard skin that shows no signs of softening or cracking. You will find winter squashes available in the supermarket year-round. Uncut squash will keep for months in a cool, dry place. Green and orange-colored winter squash can be a meal by themselves, used in soups, or stuffed with grains. Acorn and butternut are a good beginner's choice. Don't peel a squash before baking it. Simply cut in half and cook it cut-side down. Raw squash added to soups and stews will require peeling.

Tomatoes   Choose tomatoes that are firm to the touch. Store ripe tomatoes in the refrigerator. Don't bother to peel them. If you use only a portion of a tomato, store the remainder cut-side down on a ceramic or glass dish to keep it from becoming slimy.

Turnips and Rutabagas   These are close relatives, and they are interchangeable. Choose roots with firm, smooth skin, and avoid very large ones, which may be woody and pithy. It is best to peel them before using because the skin can be chewy. Like carrots, they make good snacks eaten raw. They are delicious tossed into soups or stews, steamed, sautéed, and baked. They will keep refrigerated for 1 to 2 weeks.

Yams and Sweet Potatoes   What American supermarkets call a yam is in fact a variety of sweet potato. (A true yam has a hairy, woody, brown exterior, and it is not widely available in the United States.) Do not substitute a true yam for a sweet potato. The light-color sweet potato you find in most supermarkets has a pale yellow flesh and is dry and crumbly when cooked. The darker variety sweet potato, often mislabeled as a yam, has a dark orange flesh and is sweet and moist when cooked. Look for firm, plump, blemish-free potatoes. They'll keep for a few weeks stored in a cool, dry place. Do not refrigerate them unless they are already cooked. Sweet potatoes can be peeled and eaten raw for a snack or grated and eaten raw in salads. They lend themselves to baking, boiling, and roasting. Don't peel whole sweet potatoes or yams before baking, but do peel them for stews and soups.

Soy Foods

Just as whole kernels of wheat become flour for bread, pasta, and cookies, soybeans come in a variety of forms. Look for the following soy foods as you shop.

Miso Miso is a thick puree made from the fermentation of soy beans, salt, and various grains ranging in flavor from light to hearty.

White or rice miso is mild and relatively sweet, red or barley miso is savory, and dark soy miso is thick and strongly flavored. Miso adds rich flavor to soups, spreads, stews, and sauces. You will find it in natural food stores and Asian markets.

Soy Cheese Made from soy milk, soy cheese is similar but not identical to dairy cheese. Some soy cheese has casein added to make it melt when heated, and casein is a milk product. If you are a vegan looking to avoid all animal products, read the label on the cheese before tossing it into your shopping basket. You will find soft varieties of soy cheese gently whipped into a consistency much like cream cheese, and firm cheese similar to mozzarella and Cheddar.

Soy Milk This dairy-free beverage is made by blending soaked whole soybeans with water and straining out the pulp. Use it in the same way you use cow's milk. Various brands taste surprisingly different from one another. If you don't like the first one you try, sample several others before you make a final decision about whether soy milk is for you. In cooked food—such as soup—there is little taste difference between soy milk and cow's milk. Lightly sweetened, plain, or vanilla soy milk is delicious poured on cereal, and it makes yummy chocolate pudding or "milk" shakes. Most soy milk is hermetically sealed to last months before opening; once opened, soy milk keeps for about 7 to 10 days in the refrigerator. Look for brands made from organic soybeans and fortified with calcium.

Soy Sauce   The best soy sauce has no sugar, food coloring, or chemical additives. Both shoyu and tamari are Japanese-type soy sauces. Shoyu contains soybeans, wheat, water, and salt. Tamari is a by-product of miso making and is saltier and more strongly flavored than shoyu, and it contains no wheat. It adds flavor and salt to soups, stews, sauces, and stir-fries. American, Japanese, and Chinese products are available in natural food stores, Asian groceries, and supermarkets.

Soy Yogurt   Cultured from soy milk and available in many flavors, soy yogurt is lactose- and cholesterol-free. It has the texture of dairy yogurt, but it does not taste the same.

Tempeh   This cultured soybean product is a fermented soybean cake with a nutty aroma and chewy texture that may remind you of meat. Marinate it in soy sauce, and then fry, grill, or steam it. Use it as a meat replacement in stir-fries or stews. Look for tempeh in most natural food stores either fresh or, more commonly, frozen. Thaw tempeh before using, but slice it while it's partially frozen to avoid crumbling.

Tofu   Tofu is a versatile food made by separating soy milk into curds and whey and pressing the curds into blocks. It has a unique custardlike consistency with little taste of its own. It readily absorbs the flavors from other ingredients, and the recipes in this book will help you turn tofu into one of your favorite fast foods. Tofu varies by firmness and texture.

Extra-firm tofu and *firm tofu* are dense and solid and are ideal for slicing, dicing, frying, and broiling. They hold up well in soups, lasagna, and spaghetti sauce. *Soft tofu* is creamy and useful for dressings, dips, shakes, and desserts.

Silken tofu has a fine, creamy consistency and is made from a slightly different process. Silken tofu is also available in extra-firm, firm, and soft. It can be used in the applications described earlier. In Japan, silken tofu is enjoyed as is with a touch of soy sauce and topped with chopped green onions.

Seasoned tofu is ready to eat straight from the package. It is a firm, dense tofu product produced by extracting the water under pressure and cooking the solids with soy sauce and spices. Use it in sandwiches and savory dishes.

Tofu is usually found in the produce section of the supermarket, although some stores sell tofu in the dairy or deli sections. It is most commonly sold in water-filled tubs, vacuum packs, or aseptic packages. Check the expiration date on the package, and buy tofu as far ahead of the expiration date as possible.

Store aseptic packages of tofu in a cool place or the refrigerator. Once an aseptic package is opened, refrigerate unused portions in an air-tight container, and use within 2 days.

Store water-filled tubs in the refrigerator. Opened water-packed tofu can be stored for a week if it is covered and the water changed daily. If tofu becomes slimy or sour, throw it away.

Store seasoned tofu in the refrigerator. *Do not rinse and cover seasoned tofu with water.*

Here's a chart to help you determine how best to keep your tofu fresh:

	BEFORE OPENING		AFTER OPENING	
	Store in Refrigerator	Store in Cupboard	Rinse and Cover with Fresh Water	Store Covered in Refrigerator
Water-Filled Tubs	X		X	X
Vacuum Packs	X		X	X
Aseptic Packages		X		X
Seasoned Tofu	X			X

Depending on the dish you're making, you may want to make water-packed tofu firmer by pressing out some of the water. Pressed water-packed tofu grills beautifully and picks up more flavor in stir-fries. Strange as the pressing process may sound, give it a try. Sandwich the tofu between two plates. Weight the top plate with a heavy book. (Sometimes the top plate slides off during the pressing process, so keep the plates away from the edge of a counter or table.) After 15 to 30 minutes, remove the weight and top plate, and drain the water from the bottom plate. The tofu is now ready to slice and use.

Breads and Grains

Store whole grain bread, corn tortillas, whole wheat flour, brown rice, oatmeal, and most other grains in your refrigerator or freezer. They will last longer, and you won't find your supplies invaded by mold or insects. Single slices of frozen bread thaw in minutes, and if you're in a hurry, pop the bread into a toaster.

Shopping List

Shopping with a list can save you time and energy. Organize your list by type of item; this simplifies your path through the store. Keep a running list of basics; when you get low on an item, add it to the list. Here is a list of basic supplies to have on hand that will keep you cooking if there is a blizzard, you've got 2 days of nonstop exams, or you are sick and need to fend for yourself.

Breads and Grains

☐ Baked chips

☐ Brown rice

☐ Cornmeal

☐ Flour (whole grain and white)

☐ Oatmeal

☐ Rice cakes

☐ Tortillas

☐ Whole grain breads

☐ Whole grain pasta

☐ Whole grain pocket bread

☐ Whole grain, ready-to-eat cereal

Commercially Prepared Food

☐ Canned beans (black, garbanzo, kidney, pinto, refried)

☐ Canned whole tomatoes

☐ Chili

☐ Soup

☐ Pasta sauce

Fresh Produce

☐ Apples

☐ Bananas

☐ Bell peppers

☐ Carrots

☐ Garlic

☐ Lemons

☐ Lettuce

☐ Onions

☐ Oranges

☐ Potatoes

☐ Sweet potatoes

☐ Tomatoes

☐ Winter squash

Nuts, Seeds, Dried Beans, and Dried Fruit

☐ Dried beans (kidney and pinto)

☐ Dried split peas

☐ Figs

☐ Lentils

☐ Natural nut butters (refrigerate)

- ☐ Raisins
- ☐ Tahini (sesame seed butter; refrigerate)
- ☐ Unsalted nuts

Condiments
- ☐ Fruit spreads
- ☐ Maple syrup
- ☐ Mustard
- ☐ Salsa
- ☐ Soy sauce
- ☐ Tabasco
- ☐ Vinegar

Oil
- ☐ Canola oil
- ☐ Olive oil
- ☐ Toasted sesame oil

Refrigerated Items
- ☐ Cheese
- ☐ Eggs
- ☐ Lowfat yogurt
- ☐ Miso
- ☐ Soy milk or lowfat dairy milk
- ☐ Tofu

Frozen Foods
- ☐ Corn
- ☐ Peas

Beverages
- ☐ Coffee
- ☐ Juice
- ☐ Tea

CHAPTER 2

Tools, Techniques, and Terms

Secrets Revealed

Most people learn how to cook through trial and error. Don't let cooking intimidate you. It's really very simple: You just apply heat over time, and things cook. There's much more latitude in cooking than you might think, and numbers are fairly arbitrary. If you like carrots, add more. If you don't like mushrooms, use fewer. Taste as you go to learn how different ingredients add flavor to your cooking. As you become familiar with recipes, you won't feel the need to measure each 1/4 teaspoon of basil or 1/2 cup of chopped bell pepper. You will find many vegetarian recipes begin with cutting an onion, mincing a clove of garlic, or sautéing vegetables for 3 to 5 minutes. This simple process can make the difference between food that is disappointing or simply delicious. With a little experience, cooking will become more creative and faster. Finally, it's just food, and it can't bite back.

People have managed for centuries to put elaborate meals on the table with little more than one pot, a skillet, a bowl, a knife, a spoon, a spatula, and some source of heat. You can, too. You don't need fancy equipment to prepare delicious vegetarian meals.

A Few Helpful Tools

Knives   You'll need a big knife (one that comfortably fits your hand) and a small paring knife for peeling and finer cuts. A good knife can be expensive, but it lasts a lifetime. (Sharpening knives is best done by hand rather than a machine. A few strokes across a steel—a metal rod with a finely ridged surface—keeps the edge sharp.)

Pans   A 10-inch skillet is an ideal size to have on hand. Many chefs stand by indestructible cast iron pans and stainless steel skillets. Some cooks prefer nonstick cookware because it requires significantly less oil for cooking and makes cleaning up easier and faster. However, recent warnings about the possible danger of a chemical used in making nonstick cookware may persuade you not to use it.

Pots   Buy a 3-quart or 4-quart pot with a lid. If you're a minimalist, this one pot is a suitable tool for performing most cooking functions. You may also need a larger pot if you're going to cook big batches of pasta or homemade chili. Get the best pots you can afford. Flimsy, thin-bottom cookware heats food unevenly and causes it to burn. Avoid aluminum pots because aluminum can leach into your food.

Miscellaneous Tools   Here is a list of additional helpful items:

baking dish
colander
cutting board, wooden
dishcloths, two
dish towels, two
handheld can opener—not electric (The Swing-A-Way brand
    is a good bet at about $8.)
handheld grater

measuring spoons (If you don't have measuring spoons,
a regular teaspoon works fine. Three teaspoons equal
one tablespoon.)
mixing bowl
pot holders, two
potato masher
slotted long-handled spoon
slotted spatula
vegetable steamer basket or pot

Cutting Up Food

Knowing a few basic principles will help you cook efficiently
and make food taste great; good cooks soon attract hungry
spectators around their kitchen table.

To reduce preparation time and to wield your knife like
the cooks you see on TV, use a sharp knife. A knife is much
more likely to slip and cut you if it is dull, and the food may
turn out looking like it was run over by a bicycle tire.

For most cutting, hold the food in place with one hand,
curling your fingers slightly back so that no fingertips are left
sticking out for the knife to find. Hold the knife with your
thumb and first finger on either side of the blade.

Don't always cut things into tiny pieces. Cut larger
pieces, when possible, to save time. Use large chunks for stews
and smaller cuts for salads and stir-fries. Whenever appropri-
ate, use unpeeled fruits and vegetables. To make cutting
round food easy, first slice off a small portion to create a flat
surface. Place the cut side down, and begin slicing pieces.

Know Your Terms

Chiffonade   This is a way to cut large flat leaves like spinach
and kale. Crumple and rumple the leaves into a ball, and
hold them together with one hand while you cut with your

other hand. Another method is to roll the leaves from end to end and slice into thin strips.

Chop   Cut foods into pieces about 1/2-inch square.

Dice or Finely Chop   Cut slices crosswise in each direction to create cubes or pieces ranging in size from 1/8 inch to 1/4 inch. To speed things up, bundle slices together and cut through the pile.

Grate   Use a low-tech multisided grater to grate fresh vegetables and cheese for small salads and other meals. Grated foods add an interesting texture and lightness to dishes.

Mince   Garlic and gingerroot are commonly minced. Very small pieces tend to jump and scatter. Use the knife blade to push the pieces back into a heap to make cutting easier.

Slice   Make cuts about 1/2 inch apart for thick slices, 1/8 to 1/4 inch for thinner slices.

Cooking Terms

Baking and Roasting   What's the difference? There isn't any. Both terms describe preparing food with dry heat in an oven. Baking or roasting usually takes longer than most other cooking methods. Remember to preheat the oven so that it will be the right temperature when you are ready to begin cooking. This is especially important when baking cakes, breads, and cookies. Preheating also speeds up the cooking process.

Boiling and Simmering   Boiled foods cook in rapidly agitating liquid with bubbles breaking on the surface. Simmering involves more gently moving liquid, cooking just below the boiling point.

Braising This is simmering foods in a small amount of liquid. Use vegetable stock, wine, soy sauce, or juices as all or part of the liquid to increase the flavor of the finished dish. Add salt toward the end of cooking because salt concentrates as the liquids evaporate.

Broiling Broiling involves cooking in a preheated oven, with food approximately 3 to 4 inches from the heat. This method is fast and requires close attention because the heat is high and foods can quickly burn. Leave the oven door slightly ajar so you can see what's happening.

Microwaving Microwaves are good for reheating food and cooking a limited number of dishes. (For truly wonderful-tasting meals, use some other cooking method.) Never put metal items inside a microwave because they can cause dangerous sparking. If this happens, switch the oven off at once. Never turn the oven on when it is empty; microwaves may bounce off the walls and damage the cavity.

Sautéing Sautéing is a quick cooking method done on top of the stove. Food usually cooks in oil on medium or medium-high heat. Making sure the heat isn't too high can head off trouble. Heat the oil in the skillet before adding the food, and the food will absorb less of it. To *sauté until soft* means to cook until the food is tender but not browned. To *sauté until brown* means to cook gently until the food is golden. A flavorful sauté is what gives real body to different dishes. It may seem like the liquid and starchy ingredients form the "base" or "soul" of pot foods like stews, soups, and beans, but actually they are more the medium that holds the bright flavors of your sauté.

Steaming Hot vapor produced by simmering or boiling water in a tightly covered pot cooks the food. Use a two-piece steaming pot or stainless steel steaming basket inserted into a pot with a tight-fitting lid. Keep the water level lower than the bottom of the steamer to avoid sogginess. Let the water come to a boil, and then add the vegetables. Properly steamed vegetables are crisp and tender with good color.

Steaming times for vegetables will vary according to variety and cut sizes. Most vegetables cook in a matter of minutes. Brussels sprouts, cabbage, and cauliflower overcook quickly. You will know because your kitchen will start to stink. When preparing vegetables that require longer cooking, check the water level and add more water if it is boiling away. When you open the pot, tilt the lid so that the rising steam will move away from you.

Stir-Frying Stir-frying is the Asian version of a hot, fast cooking technique. One of the advantages to this type of cooking is that you can cook a whole meal and use only one skillet or wok.

Chop and slice the vegetables and measure the seasoning before starting. Line up all of your ingredients near the stove. Heat a small amount of oil in a hot skillet, and then add the garlic, the seasonings for flavoring the whole dish, and vegetables a handful at a time. When cooking with garlic on high heat, keep an eye on it, because garlic burns easily. Avoid overcrowding the pan; otherwise you'll end up with soggy food. Begin by tossing in the hard vegetables first and progress to softer vegetables. Always keep the food in motion—stir and fry. The last things you add are liquid seasonings, like soy sauce. Remove the vegetables from the pan quickly to maintain crispness.

Never immerse a hot pan in cold water—this can warp the metal. Let the pan cool slightly, then add water.

Season to Taste

Research in the fields of chemistry and psychology suggests that specific aromas can increase brain power and the ability to concentrate. A study at the University of Cincinnati demonstrated that people in a room scented with peppermint had more correct answers to test questions than people taking the same test in unscented rooms. So take a deep breath when you season food in the kitchen. As you experiment, you'll learn how different seasonings and foods naturally go together. The more you use seasonings, the more your seasoning sense will become second nature.

Herbs and Spices

For starters, begin with a few basic dried herbs and spices: basil, cinnamon, cumin, curry, mint, oregano, rosemary, and thyme. It is best to buy herbs and spices in the smallest possible amounts, and store them in tightly closed bottles in a cool, dry spot out of direct light. Replace seasonings after 6 months to a year when their aroma and taste have faded. When substituting dried herbs for fresh ones, use about one-third the amount called for in the recipe. When increasing a recipe, don't increase the seasonings as drastically as the main ingredients. Make small changes, and taste. Sprinkle spices and herbs from your hand or a measuring spoon into a steaming pot, not from the bottle. Steam introduced into the bottle will hasten the loss of flavor and aroma.

Cilantro and parsley are two herbs that must be fresh. Dried parsley tastes like straw, and dried cilantro doesn't resemble the fresh version at all. Most people love fresh cilantro, but taste it before you toss a handful into something you're cooking. Substitute parsley if you don't like cilantro.

Sophisticated Tastes

Condiments from around the globe, once found only in expensive gourmet grocery stores, are now on the shelves of well-stocked supermarkets; they bring instant, striking flavor to meals. Use chutney to jazz up plain baked potatoes, winter squash, and bagels. If you like your food "hot 'n' spicy," Szechwan sauce and Vietnamese red chili sauce can perk up main dish meals. Hoisin sauce, often called the catsup of Asia, is a popular table condiment for a variety of dishes, including stir-fries. It is made from soy sauce, garlic, and chiles with the sweet flavor of anise. Hoisin sauce is a great marinade for tofu. A splash of vinegar gives oven-roasted potatoes, cooked vegetables, soup, and even a pot of beans a wonderful boost. Tahini, made from ground sesame seeds, adds interesting flavor to many dishes and dips. A few drops of toasted sesame oil gives stir-fries and cooked vegetables real character. It costs about $4, but its powerful flavor makes a small bottle last a long time. Don't forget the ever-popular salsa, Tabasco, catsup, and mustard for flavoring food.

CHAPTER 3

Breakfast
Anytime

On most mornings, cold cereal or a bagel will do, but when you're ready for more, wake up to Overnight Oatmeal—it "cooks" while you sleep. Stir up a quick tofu scramble, or sdelight your friends with a Beer Pancake brunch. You will find ideas in this chapter that are satisfying any time of the day.

Open-Face Omelet

PREPARATION TIME: 15 minutes

This is so delicious! It's a great way to use up bits of vegetables. You need about 2 cups of vegetables for 2 eggs. The Sesame Sauce takes only minutes to prepare, and it's worth making to see the magic the cornstarch performs. Serve the omelet with a cup of hot tea and fragrant tangerine slices.

1/2 cup onions, thinly sliced (about 1/4 medium onion)
1 tablespoon vegetable oil
1 cup bean sprouts (the white ones with the tiny pale
    yellow-green heads)
6 to 8 snow peas, thinly sliced (about 1/4 cup)
1/4 cup celery, thinly sliced (about 1/4 medium stalk)
2 eggs
1/2 teaspoon soy sauce
1/2 teaspoon fresh ginger, finely minced

Sesame Sauce
1/2 cup water
1 tablespoon soy sauce
1/4 teaspoon toasted sesame oil
1 green onion, finely chopped
2 teaspoons cornstarch
2 teaspoons cool water

1. In a medium skillet on medium-high heat, sauté the onion in the oil for 3 to 4 minutes, until translucent. Add bean sprouts, snow peas, and celery; continue to sauté for 3 to 4 minutes.
2. In a bowl, whisk together the eggs, soy sauce, and ginger.

3. When the vegetables are crisp-tender, pour the eggs over the vegetables. Cook on low heat until the egg mixture is golden on one side, about 3 minutes. Cut egg "pancake" in half with a spatula, and turn each piece. Cook until the undersides are golden and the eggs are set, about 3 minutes.

4. While the omelet cooks, make the sauce. In a small saucepan, bring 1/2 cup water, soy sauce, sesame oil, and green onion to a boil. Dissolve the cornstarch in cool water, and stir it into the simmering sauce. Continue stirring until the sauce thickens. Remove from heat.

Serve omelet with a splash of Sesame Sauce, or if preferred, sprinkle with soy sauce and chopped green onions, or sprinkle with sesame seeds.

NOTE: You can substitute the following vegetables for the snow peas or celery: mushrooms, bok choy, broccoli, green peas, or bell pepper.

Makes two servings

Fried Egg Taco

This breakfast is ready to go in minutes. For a big meal, add a side dish of beans and a slice of melon.

1/4 cup commercial salsa
1/2 small tomato, chopped
1 teaspoon chopped fresh cilantro or parsley
1 egg
1 teaspoon vegetable oil
1 corn tortilla

Extras (Optional)
Black or green olives
Grated cheese
Green onion, chopped
Mild green chiles, canned

1. In a small saucepan, heat salsa, tomato, and cilantro until warm, but not simmering.

2. Fry the egg in a small, lightly oiled skillet on medium-high heat until well set on the bottom, about 1 minute; then cover the pan and cook until the egg is completely set (the white will no longer be clear).

3. Heat a corn tortilla in a heavy skillet on medium-high until just beginning to brown, about 30 seconds.

4. Place warm tortilla on a plate. Top with egg and salsa mixture. Sprinkle on your choice of extras; fold and eat.

Makes one serving

Fifteen-Minute
French Toast

PREPARATION TIME: 5 minutes

COOKING TIME: 3 to 4 minutes per pancake

If you're looking for a quick breakfast, soak the bread in the batter the night before, cover, and refrigerate until morning. They take just a few minutes to cook.

1/2 cup soy milk or dairy milk
1 egg
1/4 teaspoon vanilla
1/4 teaspoon ground cinnamon
1 teaspoon sugar (optional)
4 slices multigrain bread
2 teaspoons vegetable oil

1. In a shallow pan or bowl, whisk together the milk, egg, vanilla, cinnamon, and sugar.

2. Dip the slices of bread into the milk mixture one by one, turning to coat both sides.

3. Heat a lightly oiled, medium skillet on medium heat, and fry the bread until it is lightly browned on both sides. Serve topped with maple syrup, sliced fruit, applesauce, or your favorite fruit spread.

Makes two servings

Fluffy Vegan Pancakes

PREPARATION TIME: 4 minutes

COOKING TIME: 3 to 4 minutes per pancake

This eggless recipe makes light, fluffy pancakes due to whipping the liquid ingredients with a fork for 1 minute until frothy.

1 cup whole wheat flour
1 cup unbleached white flour
1 tablespoon baking powder
2 cups soy milk
1 tablespoon vegetable oil

1. Stir the flour and baking powder together in a large bowl. In a separate bowl, combine the soy milk and oil, and whip for about 1 minute. Pour the soy mixture into the flour mixture. Stir just to combine. Don't worry about lumps.

2. Lightly oil a medium skillet. Heat over medium heat. When a few drops of water sprinkled on the skillet sizzle or bead up, the pan is ready.

3. For each pancake, pour 1/2 cup of the batter onto the skillet. Cook until the pancakes begin to bubble, about 3 minutes. Turn with a spatula, and cook until the underside is lightly browned. Serve with maple syrup.

NOTE: If you like thin pancakes, add more soy milk a tablespoon at a time.

Makes two servings

Beer Pancakes

PREPARATION TIME: 5 minutes

COOKING TIME: About 3 minutes for each pancake

Eat these intriguing pancakes for breakfast or dessert.

1³/₄ cups whole wheat flour
1¹/₂ teaspoons baking powder
¹/₂ teaspoon baking soda
1 egg
3 tablespoons vegetable oil
1 tablespoon honey
1 can or bottle (12 ounces) beer

1. In a large bowl, combine the flour, baking powder, and baking soda, and mix well. In another bowl, whisk together the egg, oil, and honey with a fork.

2. Add the liquid mixture and the beer to the dry ingredients; stir just until a smooth batter is formed. The batter will be somewhat lumpy and slightly thick.

3. Lightly oil a medium skillet, and place it over medium heat until hot. Pour ¹/₂ cup of the batter at a time onto the skillet. Cook the pancakes until the bottoms are golden brown and the tops begin to bubble. Flip them over, and cook until the undersides are golden brown. Serve with maple syrup.

Makes two or three servings

Hot Stovetop Oatmeal

Steaming oatmeal properly prepared is a hearty, early morning meal. This version is sweetened with strawberry preserves and uses old-fashioned rolled oats.

$1/2$ cup rolled oats
1 cup water
$1/8$ to $1/4$ teaspoon salt
2 teaspoons strawberry preserves (or more if you like)
2 tablespoons chopped walnuts or almonds

Extras (Optional)
Sliced bananas
Fresh or frozen berries
Raisins, dates, currants
A dash of cinnamon, nutmeg, or cardamom
Warm Apple Slices (page 223)
Chopped walnuts or almonds

1. In a small pot with a tight-fitting lid, bring the oats, water, and salt to a boil. Lower heat to medium-low, and continue to cook, stirring for about 5 minutes.

2. Remove from heat and stir in the preserves. Cover and let sit for 2 to 3 minutes.

3. Serve the oatmeal sprinkled with nuts, along with any of the optional items listed. If you desire, top with a splash of soy or dairy milk.

Variation: Omit the preserves and substitute maple syrup or brown sugar when you serve the dish.

NOTE: Do not use "quick-cooking or "instant" oatmeal. It turns to glue. Fill the empty pot with water as soon as you serve the oatmeal, and let it soak while you eat. The oatmeal that sticks to the sides of the pot will slide right off when it's clean-up time.

Makes one serving

Overnight Oatmeal

PREPARATION TIME: 4 minutes

Watching the sugar melt on a bowl of hot oatmeal fresh off the stove is a heavenly sight, but on those mornings when you're too busy to cook, wake up to oatmeal ready and waiting in the refrigerator.

1 cup old-fashioned rolled oats
1 cup soy milk or dairy milk
1 tablespoon raisins
1/2 teaspoon ground cinnamon
1/2 to 1 cup chopped seasonal fruit (optional)

1. In a cereal bowl, combine the oats, milk, raisins, and cinnamon. Cover and refrigerate overnight.
2. In the morning stir in fresh fruit, if you desire, and breakfast is ready. Serve it chilled.

Makes one or two servings

Scrambled Tofu Curry

PREPARATION TIME: 7 minutes

Tofu scrambles are quick and versatile. Serve this dish with a slice of whole grain toast and a glass of chilled orange juice for a great start to the day.

5 ounces firm or extra-firm tofu (packaged in tubs of water)
1 teaspoon vegetable oil
1 tablespoon finely sliced scallion
1 tablespoon diced green or red bell pepper
2 tablespoons diced carrot
1/4 teaspoon curry powder
Salt and pepper

1. In a shallow bowl or plate, lightly mash the tofu with a fork so that it resembles the texture of scrambled eggs. Set it aside.

2. Heat the oil in a small skillet over medium heat. Sauté the scallion, pepper, carrot, and curry for 2 to 3 minutes, or until the vegetables begin to soften. Reduce the heat to low, and stir in the tofu; cook for about 1 minute or until the mixture is hot. Serve immediately. Salt and pepper to taste.

Makes one serving

Greek-Style
Scrambled Tofu

PREPARATION TIME: 7 minutes

Serve with hot coffee, a muffin, and crisp apple slices.

5 ounces firm or extra-firm tofu
1 teaspoon olive oil
1/4 cup chopped scallion (include green end, 1 large or
     2 small)
2 cloves garlic, minced
1/4 teaspoon dried oregano
1 cup tightly packed chopped fresh spinach
2 to 3 tablespoons crumbled feta cheese
Salt and pepper (optional)

1. In a shallow bowl or plate, lightly mash the tofu with a fork
   so that it resembles the texture of scrambled eggs. Set it
   aside.

2. Heat the oil in a medium skillet over medium heat. Sauté
   the scallion, garlic, and oregano for 30 seconds, and add the
   spinach. Cook, stirring until the spinach wilts, about 3 minutes. The water that remains on the spinach from washing
   will be enough to cook the spinach.

3. Reduce the heat to low. Add the tofu, and gently stir until the
   mixture is warm, about 1 minute. Stir in the feta cheese, and
   serve immediately. Season with salt and pepper, if you desire.

Makes one serving

Corn Cakes

PREPARATION TIME: 3 minutes

COOKING TIME: About 5 minutes per corn cake

Here is a delicious way to use leftover polenta. Serve these cakes for breakfast with maple syrup and fresh fruit, or for lunch with chunky salsa.

Cooked, cooled polenta
Vegetable oil

Cut the polenta into 1/2-inch-thick slices, about the size of your hand. Lightly oil a nonstick skillet with vegetable oil, and set it over medium-high heat until hot. Add the polenta and fry until it is warm and slightly crispy on both sides.

Makes one serving

CHAPTER 4

Dips, Spreads, and Snacks

The recipes in this chapter are premium formulas for fast food. Combine these dips and spreads with crusty bread, crackers, chips, and vegetables, and voilà, you have the makings for simple meals or great snacks. Whip up a bowl of hummus and have a feast! What could be more heavenly than guacamole scooped onto tortillas or toast? If you're in a hurry, take a moment to make one of the recipes in this chapter—it's worth it!

Salsa

PREPARATION TIME: 6 minutes

This salsa makes a delicious topping for any bean and rice dish. Salsa over plain rice with slices of ripe avocado is irresistible. And baked chips dipped in salsa is a first-class snack. Use whole canned tomatoes in the winter when fresh supermarket tomatoes are expensive. (They may even taste better.)

3 cups chopped fresh tomatoes or whole canned tomatoes,
    drained and chopped
1/2 cup chopped cilantro
3 or 4 medium chopped green onions
1 medium jalapeño chile, minced
3 tablespoons fresh lemon or lime juice
1 clove garlic, minced
Salt to taste

In a medium bowl, mix all ingredients together. You're all set.

NOTE: For the kick in your salsa, cilantro is a must. Most of the heat in chiles comes from the seeds inside. If you want to lower the fire, cut the chile lengthwise, and remove the seeds and veins. Avoid touching your eyes when cutting and deseeding chiles.

Makes about 3 cups

Tsiziki Sauce and Dip

PREPARATION TIME: 6 minutes

Dip fresh vegetables and chunks of French bread into this garlicky sauce. Use it as a dressing for green salads, grain dishes, and pocket-bread sandwiches. Adjust the number of garlic cloves to suit your taste.

1 large cucumber, peeled and finely chopped
1 cup plain nonfat yogurt
1 teaspoon dried dill weed
4 large cloves garlic, minced
1 tablespoon fresh lemon juice
Salt

Combine all the ingredients in a bowl. If you can wait, let it stand at room temperature for 20 minutes. Dive in. Store leftover sauce in the refrigerator. It will keep for 3 to 4 days.

Makes about 1 1/2 cups

Tahini Sauce

Preparation Time: 5 minutes

Drizzle this luscious sauce over a platter of steamed vegetables, or spoon it over baked sweet potatoes and grain dishes. It will keep in the refrigerator for a week or longer.

1 cup nonfat yogurt
2 teaspoons tahini
1 clove garlic, minced
1 1/2 teaspoons lemon juice
1/8 teaspoon salt
Pepper

Whisk together all of the ingredients and store it in the refrigerator.

Makes 1 cup

Guacamole–
The Real Thing

PREPARATION TIME: 5 minutes

Here is a recipe for transforming an ordinary fruit into one of the world's greatest dips. If you can use a fork, you can make guacamole ("avocado sauce"). Use it as a dip with chips or as a topping for burritos, tacos, and quesadillas.

1 avocado (slightly overripe works best)
1 tablespoon fresh lemon or lime juice (to prevent browning)
Tabasco
$1/8$ teaspoon salt (optional)

1. Slice the avocado in half lengthwise, and gently twist to remove the seed. Make lengthwise and crosswise cuts into the flesh every $1/2$ inch. Scoop the avocado cubes into a bowl. Mash the avocado with a fork and stir in lemon or lime juice.
2. Add a splash of Tabasco, and salt to taste.

Makes about 1 cup

Eggplant and
Garlic Spread

PREPARATION TIME: 10 minutes

COOKING TIME: About 20 minutes

*Make this dish into a hearty meal surrounded with toasted pita
bread and fresh vegetables for dipping, or spread it on crusty French
bread for a creamy open-faced sandwich. Broiling an eggplant is as
simple as deflating a balloon. It is done cooking when the eggplant
is completely wrinkled, limp, and soft.*

1 eggplant (about 1 pound)
2 tablespoons tahini
2 tablespoons fresh lemon juice
1 large clove garlic, finely minced
2 tablespoons minced onion
Salt and pepper
1 teaspoon olive oil (optional)
1 tablespoon minced fresh parsley (optional)

Preheat the broiler.

1. Prick the eggplant in several places with a fork, and cut off
   the stem end. Place the eggplant on a baking sheet, and
   broil for 20 minutes or until done, turning the vegetable several times so that the skin chars on all sides.

2. When the eggplant is cool enough to handle, cut it in half; scrape out the flesh into a bowl. Discard the skin, and mash the eggplant with a potato masher or fork. Add the tahini, lemon juice, garlic, onion, and salt and pepper to taste.

3. If you have time, cover the spread and refrigerate it for a few hours. Before serving, sprinkle it with oil and parsley if you desire.

Makes about 1¹/₂ cups

Roasted Garlic

PREPARATION TIME: 4 minutes

COOKING TIME: About 60 minutes

Once cooked, garlic's strong smell disappears, and the flavor becomes sweet and buttery. Use it to replace mayonnaise on sandwiches, spread it on slices of crusty sourdough bread, or use it on baked potatoes and pizza. To eat it, gently squeeze the large end of the cooked clove, and the garlic will slip out of the shell.

3 heads of garlic

Preheat the oven to 350 degrees F.

1. Carefully remove the outer papery skin from the garlic heads. Leave the heads intact, and do not break them apart into cloves.
2. Carefully cut the top 1/4 inch off of each head. Arrange the garlic heads in a small baking dish without crowding.
3. Add enough water to cover the bottom of the dish with 1/4 inch of water. Cover with a lid or seal the dish with foil and bake for about 60 minutes until the cloves are soft to the touch. Roasted garlic will last for at least a week in a covered container in the refrigerator.

Makes about 1/8 cup

Hummus

Hummus is a rich pâté made from garbanzo beans. If you've never eaten hummus, you're in for a classic treat. Spread it on whole grain bread to make a superior sandwich piled high with greens, tomatoes, and sliced red onions, or create an entire meal around a plateful of hummus with warm pocket bread for dipping, and a salad on the side. Hummus will keep for several days in a covered container in the refrigerator.

1 (15-ounce) can garbanzo beans, drained (about 1½ cups)
6 to 7 tablespoons fresh lemon juice (1 large or 2 small)
2 cloves garlic, minced
2 tablespoons tahini
2 tablespoons minced onion
Salt (optional)
2 tablespoons minced fresh parsley (optional)

1. Mash the garbanzo beans into a thick paste using a masher, fork, or blender. Add the lemon juice, garlic, tahini, onion, and parsley if you wish; stir.

2. Hummus should have a consistency similar to mayonnaise. If it seems too thick, add more lemon juice, 1 tablespoon at a time. Season with salt to taste and add parsley, if you desire.

Makes about 1¾ cups

Toasted Nori

PREPARATION TIME: 1 minute

Nori is a sea vegetable best known as a wrapper for sushi. When you have a snack attack, here's a 1-minute fix. This chip is a delicacy that you won't eat by the handfuls, but will nibble and savor.

1 sheet nori
Toasted sesame oil
Salt

Heat a sheet of nori until it becomes fragrant, about 30 seconds, by waving it over, but not on, a burner on medium-high heat. Remove from the heat, and rub the sheet with a few drops of toasted sesame oil. Sprinkle with salt. You'll have a large, crisp "chip."

Makes one serving

Popping Ideas!

Store popcorn in an airtight container in a cool place, or refrigerate. Water inside the corn kernel is what helps popcorn explode when it's heated. If you have trouble with unpopped kernels when you make popcorn, put the popcorn in a jar and add water. Let it soak for a few minutes and drain. Shake the jar to moisten all the kernels. Put a lid on the jar. The popcorn will be ready to use the next day.

Popcorn Fundamentals

An air popper is the easiest method for making popcorn. If you don't have one, use a pot. In a 6-quart heavy-bottomed pot, heat 1 tablespoon of olive oil on medium heat with 1/2 cup of popcorn. Cover with a lid slightly ajar to allow steam to escape. When the corn begins to pop, shake the pot until the popping almost stops. Remove from heat and wait for the kernels to stop popping before removing the lid.

Flavoring

If you're a plain buttered-popcorn-with-salt sort of person, you know what to do next. If you want something different, try one of these flavors. Whatever you choose, the important thing to add is salt; it brings out the taste.

Parmesan Popcorn

Sauté two cloves of minced garlic in 1 to 2 tablespoons olive oil on medium-high heat for about 1 minute. Pour the oil and garlic over the popcorn, and add Parmesan cheese and salt. Mix thoroughly. Taste. Add more salt if necessary.

Hot Chili Popcorn

Sauté two cloves of minced garlic in 2 tablespoons of olive oil on medium-high heat for about 1 minute. Add 1 teaspoon cumin powder and 1 teaspoon chili powder to oil and stir for a few seconds to combine. Pour oil mixture over popcorn. Add salt, mix thoroughly, and enjoy.

CHAPTER 5

Soups and Stews

Forget the idea that homemade soup takes hours to prepare. Although opening a can of soup is convenient, the soups you will find here are surprisingly quick to make. Minute Miso Soup is good for breakfast and dinner. Impulse Minestrone is ready in 10 minutes, and if you like soup thick and creamy, you'll enjoy Corn and Potato Chowder. "A good soup gathers chairs," so invite your friends, and ask them to bring the bread.

Minute Miso Soup

PREPARATION TIME: 6 minutes

Miso is a concentrated, fermented pâté made from soybeans, with the consistency of creamy peanut butter. It makes a delicate, clear soup in minutes. A cup of miso soup can be a satisfying one-bowl pick-me-up when you want something warm to take the chill out of a night of studying, or it can be a quick breakfast. In Japan, it's part of the traditional morning meal along with rice.

You will find miso in Japanese and Chinese markets, natural food stores, and some supermarkets. It keeps almost indefinitely in the refrigerator. Miso comes in many flavors. For starters try red miso, barley miso, or Hatcho miso.

Sip a modest cup of miso soup, or try an extravagant version with tofu and onions. The variations on this soup are endless. Just remember, for best results use vegetables in small amounts and cook them only slightly.

2 cups water
4 onion slices, cut into very thin half moons
1/4 cup carrots, cut into thin matchsticks
1/4 cup tofu, cut into small cubes
1 tablespoon miso
Dash of pepper
1 tablespoon chopped scallion (optional)

1. Combine the water, onion, and carrots in a small covered saucepan, and simmer for 3 to 5 minutes. Add the tofu.

2. Place the miso in a cup with about 1/4 cup of the cooking liquid. Mix until all the miso is dissolved; add it to the soup. Do not boil after the miso is added. (High heat destroys miso's beneficial enzymes.) Season with pepper and garnish with scallions if you desire.

Makes two servings

Impulse Minestrone Soup

PREPARATION TIME: 15 minutes

This soup always turns out wonderfully, and it never needs to be the same. Start with one can each of tomatoes and beans and add from there. If you are using frozen vegetables, buy them in bags rather than boxes. It's easier to scoop out the amount you need.

1 teaspoon olive oil
1 large clove garlic, finely chopped
1/2 medium zucchini, sliced (about 1 cup)
1/2 teaspoon dried basil
1/8 teaspoon dried oregano
1 cup frozen mixed vegetables
1 cup canned kidney beans, drained
1 (141/2-ounce) can diced tomatoes, undrained
1 cup water
2 cups uncooked spiral pasta
Salt and pepper
Grated Parmesan (optional)

1. Heat the oil in a medium saucepan on medium heat. Sauté the garlic, zucchini, basil, and oregano, and cook, stirring, for 2 to 3 minutes. Add the mixed vegetables, beans, tomatoes, and water. Simmer for 10 minutes.

2. While the soup warms, cook the pasta in a small saucepan of boiling water for 7 to 9 minutes. Drain. Add the pasta to the soup.

3. Remove the soup from the heat and serve. Season with salt and pepper to taste. Sprinkle with grated Parmesan if you desire.

Makes two servings

Split Pea Soup

Preparation Time: 18 minutes

Cooking Time: About 40 minutes

Here chipotle chiles are used to add a hot, smoky flavor to the soup. You'll find chipotle chiles in cans packed in adobo sauce in the Mexican section of the supermarket. Wash your hands after cutting chiles because they can cause a burning sensation on your skin. Store leftover chiles in a container in the freezer.

2 teaspoons olive oil
1 cup chopped onion (1 small)
2 large cloves garlic, minced
2 medium carrots, sliced (about 2 cups)
4 cups water
1 cup dried, green split peas
2 chipotle chiles, chopped (optional)
1 large potato, cubed into $1/2$-inch pieces (about 2 cups)
$1/4$ teaspoon salt

1. Heat the oil in a 3- to 4-quart saucepan; sauté the onion and garlic on medium heat until the onion is tender, about 5 minutes, stirring occasionally. Add the carrots and continue cooking and stirring occasionally for another 3 to 5 minutes. Add the water, peas, and chipotles (if desired).

2. Cover the pot and bring it to a boil. Reduce the heat to low and simmer, covered, until the peas are tender (about 30 minutes), stirring occasionally.

3. When the peas are tender, add the potatoes to the pot and cook until they are tender, about 15 minutes. Add the salt. Serve with slices of crusty multigrain bread.

NOTE: Prepare the soup without the chipotle chiles, and it's still delicious—simply season to taste with salt and pepper.

Makes four servings

Barley Mushroom Soup

PREPARATION TIME: 20 minutes

COOKING TIME: About 45 minutes

This recipe turns water, barley, and a few vegetables into a satisfying, thick soup. It is amazing what a slow, 10-minute sauté can do to flavor the simplest ingredients. A pound of barley costs about $0.75 and can make four big pots of soup.

1 tablespoon chopped dried shiitake mushrooms (about 2)
1/2 cup hot water for soaking mushrooms
1 tablespoon olive oil
1 cup chopped onion (about 1 small)
4 fresh mushrooms, sliced (about 1 cup)
1 cup thinly sliced carrot (about 1)
1 stalk celery, thinly sliced (about 1/2 cup)
1/2 cup pearl barley
2 tablespoons flour
3 cups water
1/2 teaspoon salt
Pepper

1. Soften the shiitake mushrooms in hot water for 10 minutes, and then dice the mushrooms. Reserve the soaking liquid. Heat the oil in a 3- or 4-quart pot over medium heat. Add the shiitake mushrooms, onions, fresh mushrooms, carrot, celery, and barley. Sauté on medium-low heat for about 10 minutes, stirring frequently so the vegetables and barley do not burn. Keep an eye on the bottom of the pot and reduce the heat if the sauté is sticking or browning too quickly.

2. Add the flour, stirring continually for 1 minute. Immediately add 3 cups of water and the mushroom soaking liquid. Scrape the bottom of the pot with a big spoon to incorporate any flour that may stick to the bottom. This step is important because the flavor from the sauté is in the stuff that may be on the bottom of the pot. Continue scraping and stirring until the bottom of the pot feels smooth, about 1 minute.

3. Add the salt. Bring to a boil, then reduce the heat. Cover and simmer for about 45 minutes or until the barley is tender. Stir the pot occasionally as the soup cooks. Taste for seasoning, and add salt and pepper if necessary.

Makes two to three servings

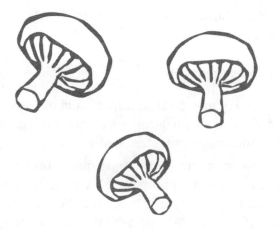

Corn and Potato Chowder

Preparation Time: 10 minutes

Cooking Time: About 20 minutes

This easy-to-prepare chowder has the richness of a creamed soup without the cream.

1 tablespoon olive oil
1 cup small onion, chopped (about 1 cup)
2 medium stalks celery, thinly sliced (about 1 cup)
2 to 3 medium russet potatoes, cut into 1/2-inch cubes
     (about 4 cups)
3 1/4 cups soy milk or lowfat dairy milk
1 cup frozen corn kernels, thawed
1/2 cup frozen peas, thawed (optional)
1/4 teaspoon salt
Pepper
Minced fresh parsley (optional)

1. Heat the oil in a 3- to 4-quart saucepan. Add the onion and celery and sauté over medium heat until the vegetables soften, 7 to 8 minutes, stirring frequently.

2. Add the potatoes and milk. Cover and simmer until the potatoes are tender, about 20 minutes. Mash some of the potatoes in the pot with a potato masher to thicken the soup. Add the corn kernels. If you like peas, add them, too. Cook just until heated through, 1 to 2 minutes. Add the salt, and season with pepper to taste.

3. Ladle the soup into a bowl, and sprinkle with parsley if you desire.

Makes three servings

Tomato Ravioli Soup

PREPARATION TIME: 6 minutes

COOKING TIME: 45 minutes

Ladle this bright red soup over plump ravioli for a new taste. It will make you smile.

2 teaspoons olive oil
1/2 medium onion, finely chopped (about 1 cup)
2 cloves garlic, finely chopped
1/2 teaspoon dried thyme
2 (14 1/2-ounce) cans chopped tomatoes, undrained
1 medium fresh tomato, chopped
1 1/2 teaspoons honey
1/2 cup water
Salt and pepper
12 fresh or frozen cheese, spinach, or squash ravioli, cooked
1 tablespoon chopped fresh parsley (optional)

1. Heat the oil in a 3- to 4-quart pot over medium heat. Add the onion and garlic and sauté 5 to 8 minutes until the onion is soft, stirring frequently. Add thyme, canned tomatoes, fresh tomato, honey, and water. Stir.

2. Cover and simmer 45 minutes on low heat. Remove from the heat. Season to taste with salt and pepper.

3. Place 4 cooked ravioli in each serving bowl and ladle the soup over them.

NOTE: If you don't have ravioli, the soup is still delicious.

Makes three servings

Lentil Soup

PREPARATION TIME: 10 minutes

COOKING TIME: 30 minutes

Use the chop-and-toss method to make this colorful soup that serves three people for a total of about $1.00.

1/2 medium onion, chopped (about 1 cup)
1 tablespoon olive oil
1 medium unpeeled red or white potato
1/2 cup lentils
2 1/2 cups water
1 medium carrot, thinly sliced
1/2 cup fresh spinach or kale (washed and tightly packed into the cup
1 medium tomato, chopped
2 to 3 garlic cloves, finely chopped
1 teaspoon ground cumin

In a medium-size pot, sauté onion in the olive oil for about 5 minutes, until soft. Cut the potato into 1-inch cubes. Add all of the other ingredients. Cover and simmer for 30 to 35 minutes. What could be easier? Serve with a splash of Tabasco or lemon juice if you desire.

NOTE: For a quick fix, use 1 or 2 cups of frozen spinach instead of fresh spinach. Buy frozen spinach in bags for easy scooping.

Makes three servings

Beer Stew

PREPARATION TIME: 15 minutes

This is a flexible recipe. Adjust the amounts to suit your taste.

4 to 5 cups water
3 medium red potatoes cut into 1/2-inch pieces (about 3 cups)
2 teaspoons olive oil
1 medium carrot, cut into 1/4-inch slices (about 1 cup)
1/2 small onion, chopped (about 1/2 cup)
1 cup canned garbanzo beans, drained
1 teaspoon curry powder
1 cup dark ale or stout beer (about 1/2 bottle)
1/4 cup frozen peas
Salt and pepper

1. Bring the water to boil in a medium saucepan. Add the potatoes and cook until just tender, but not mushy, about 10 minutes. Drain.

2. While the potatoes cook, heat the oil in a skillet over medium heat. Add the carrot, onion, and garbanzo beans; sauté 5 to 7 minutes over medium heat, stirring frequently.

3. Drain the potatoes and add them to the vegetable mixture. Add the curry and 1/2 cup of the beer. Simmer, uncovered, for about 3 minutes. Add the remaining 1/2 cup beer and simmer another 3 minutes to allow the alcohol in the beer to boil off, leaving its flavor essence in the pot. Remove from heat and stir in the peas. Salt and pepper to taste. Serve immediately.

Makes two servings

Moroccan Stew

PREPARATION TIME: 12 minutes

COOKING TIME: 15 minutes

Serve this fragrant stew on a bed of warm couscous. If the ingredient list looks long, don't worry. The stew goes together in minutes.

2 teaspoons olive oil
3/4 cup chopped onion (about 1/2 medium)
1 1/2 cups thinly sliced cabbage
1/8 teaspoon salt
1/2 large green bell pepper or 1/2 cup zucchini, cut into strips
1/8 teaspoon ground cinnamon
1 (14-ounce) can tomatoes, undrained and chopped
3/4 cup canned garbanzo beans, drained (about 8 ounces)
1/4 cup raisins
2 teaspoons fresh lemon juice
Salt and pepper

1. Heat the oil in a medium skillet on medium heat and sauté the onion for 5 minutes. Add the cabbage and sprinkle with salt. Continue to sauté the vegetables for 5 to 6 minutes, stirring occasionally.

2. Add the bell pepper and cinnamon and sauté for 2 minutes. Stir in the tomatoes, garbanzos, and raisins. Cover and simmer for about 15 minutes.

3. Add the lemon juice. Salt and pepper to taste, and serve.

Makes two servings

CHAPTER 6

Salads and Dressings

You can practically live on salads, and there are plenty of substantial combinations to choose from here. When you mix greens, beans, and grains, you have the makings for one-dish meals. With very little preparation, you can reproduce the expensive salads found in supermarket deli cases at a fraction of the cost.

Orange Rice and Black Bean Salad combines oranges and walnuts for a surprising flavor. Pasta Salad with black beans and vegetables can easily fill the center of any plate. Middle Eastern Traditional Tabouli Salad is a must-have in your vegetarian repertoire.

Leafy green salads present a special problem. While washed lettuce is tempting, dirty lettuce shrivels in the refrigerator. If washing and drying lettuce puts a stop to your salad making, treat yourself to prewashed, packaged salad greens.

Pasta Salad

PREPARATION TIME: 10 minutes

Choose your favorite vegetables for this salad.

1 cup uncooked whole wheat spiral pasta
1 cup broccoli florets
1/2 cup frozen corn, thawed
1 cup canned black beans, washed and drained
1 small tomato, chopped (about 1/2 cup)
Parmesan cheese, grated (optional)
Avocado slices (optional)

1. Cook the pasta, uncovered, in a pot of rapidly boiling water until it is al dente (cooked with a little "tooth" or crunch), 7 to 10 minutes. Just before you drain the pasta, toss in the broccoli and cook for no more than 1 minute. Drain the pot in a colander and rinse with cool water. This stops the cooking process and keeps the vegetables crisp-tender. (When making pasta salad, the noodles are rinsed, but do not rinse noodles when making hot pasta with sauce.)

2. Combine the pasta mixture with the remaining salad ingredients in a medium bowl.

3. Dress with your favorite Italian dressing, or try Bright Lemon Vinaigrette (page 84). Serve garnished with grated Parmesan cheese or avocado slices if you desire.

Makes two servings

One Potato,
Two Potato Salad

PREPARATION TIME: 6 minutes

COOKING TIME: 12 minutes

This hearty salad sparkles with color and is a meal in itself.

4 cups water
1 cup red potato, cut into bite-size pieces
1 cup yam, peeled and cut into bite-size pieces
1 cup loosely packed, prewashed fresh spinach
6 peeled cucumber slices, about 1/8-inch thick
3 Greek olives
1 to 2 tablespoons fresh lemon juice or vinaigrette dressing
Salt and pepper

1. Bring the water to a boil in a medium saucepan. Add the potato and yam and cook in rapidly boiling water until tender but not mushy, about 7 minutes. Drain thoroughly.

2. Arrange the spinach on a plate. Top with the cooked potato and yam, cucumber slices, and olives. Squeeze fresh lemon juice over the salad, or dress with your favorite vinaigrette. Season to taste with salt and pepper.

Makes one serving

Fruit Salad

PREPARATION TIME: 6 minutes

If you are tired of chomping on apples, make a fruit salad. Once you get the hang of it, you can make a beautiful multifruit salad in minutes. Peel fruit only if necessary. Squeeze a little lemon juice onto the cut pieces—without the citrus, some fruit turns brown. Garnish with bananas just before serving; that way the bananas remain firm. You'll have a hard time keeping your housemates from snacking on fruit salad left in the refrigerator.

1 apple, cored
1 pear, cored
1 orange, peeled
1 tablespoon lemon juice
Banana slices
Yogurt (optional)
Nuts or raisins (optional)

1. Cut the apple, pear, and orange into bite-size pieces. Put the fruit into a medium bowl, drizzle with lemon juice, and gently stir.

2. Spoon fruit into a serving dish and garnish with slices of banana. If you desire, top the salad with yogurt and a sprinkle of nuts or raisins.

Makes three or four servings

Cabbage Slaw

PREPARATION TIME: 6 minutes

Humble cabbage is one of the most versatile and underrated salad ingredients. The tart yogurt is a nice contrast to the sweet fruit. This is a fine fall salad when apples and pears are luscious.

1/2 firm, ripe pear
1/2 apple
1 cup shredded green cabbage
1/4 cup raisins

Dressing
1/4 cup plain yogurt
1 teaspoon frozen orange juice concentrate
1 teaspoon honey or maple syrup

1. Core and cut the pear and apple into bite-size pieces.

2. In a medium bowl, combine the pear and apple with the cabbage and raisins.

3. In a small bowl, combine all the dressing ingredients. Pour the dressing over the cabbage mixture, and gently toss. Serve with a thick slice of multigrain bread if you wish.

Makes one serving

Green Salad with Oranges

Preparation Time: 6 minutes

This good-to-eat salad is especially satisfying in the winter when cit-rus fruit is less expensive and tomatoes cost a small fortune. It looks great and is a snap to prepare.

2 cups romaine lettuce, washed and dried
1/2 large orange, peeled and cut into bite-size pieces
1 tablespoon finely chopped red onion
Honey-Yogurt Dressing (page 85)
Salt and pepper

Tear the greens into bite-size pieces and arrange them on a plate. Top with the orange pieces, and sprinkle with the red onion. Splash with the dressing, and season with salt and pepper to taste.

Makes one serving

Radical Radish Salad

Preparation Time: 7 minutes

Don't let the simplicity of this recipe keep you from enjoying a crunchy, mildly sweet, refreshing salad.

1/4 green bell pepper
5 radishes
1 small carrot
1 teaspoon fresh parsley, chopped
Salt

Dressing
1 teaspoon honey
1 tablespoon apple cider vinegar

1. Slice the pepper lengthwise into 5 or 6 pieces, then crosswise into thin pieces. Slice radishes into rounds. Cut the carrot in half lengthwise and then thinly slice each half crosswise. Combine pepper, radishes, and carrot with parsley in a medium bowl.

2. Stir the honey into the vinegar to dissolve.

3. Toss the dressing with the salad. Add a pinch of salt.

Makes two servings

Traditional Tabouli Salad

Preparation Time: 6 minutes

Soaking Time: 15 to 20 minutes

Bulgur wheat is grain that has already been partially cooked and cracked into small pieces. This salad begins by pouring boiling water over the grain and letting it stand. You'll find bulgur wheat in the supermarket shelved near the rice. This salad happily accepts variations. If you like carrots, grate some and toss them in. Are you passionate about broccoli? Steam a few florets until crisp-tender and add them to your salad. Do you love juicy cucumbers? Chop 1/4 cup and sprinkle it into the bowl, or pitch in a few garbanzo beans. If all that sounds like too much work, simply use the following recipe as is. It's delicious.

3/4 cup water
1/2 cup cracked bulgur wheat
1 tomato, finely chopped
2 scallions, finely chopped (use whole scallions, greens and all)
1 clove garlic, minced
1/4 cup finely chopped fresh parsley
1/4 teaspoon dried mint
2 tablespoons fresh lemon juice
1/2 teaspoon olive oil
Feta cheese (optional)
Salt and pepper

1. Bring the water to a boil in a medium saucepan. Add the cracked bulgur wheat, cover, and remove the pan from the heat. Let the pot stand for 15 to 20 minutes. The bulgur will become soft and fluffy.

2. When the bulgur has absorbed the water, spoon it into a medium bowl, and add the tomato, scallions, garlic, parsley, mint, lemon juice, and olive oil.

3. If you wish, sprinkle with feta cheese just before serving. Taste and season with salt and pepper. The salad will taste best if it sits in the refrigerator for 30 minutes before serving to let the flavors mingle. If you're too hungry to wait, go for it!

Makes two servings

Marinated Vegetables

Preparation Time: 7 minutes

Marinated vegetables make satisfying snacks. They're great tossed into salads, piled on slices of bread, or eaten straight from the jar. Before placing vegetables in a marinade, first lightly steam them. Mushrooms, red onions, cucumbers, and cooked beans do not need presteaming. Marinated vegetables need to relax in the sauce for several hours before they're ready to eat. They will keep up to a week refrigerated in a tightly closed container, but they'll probably disappear long before that.

2 cups vegetables (carrots, broccoli, cauliflower, green beans,
    bell peppers)
$1/4$ cup canned garbanzo or kidney beans, drained
1 to 2 teaspoons olive oil
$1/4$ cup apple cider vinegar, wine vinegar, or balsamic vinegar
1 clove garlic, minced
$1/4$ teaspoon dried basil

1. Place the vegetables in a steamer over boiling water. Cover and steam 1 to $1 1/2$ minutes, or until the vegetables are crisp-tender but not mushy.
2. Remove from heat and quickly cool the vegetables under cold water for about 30 seconds.
3. Place the vegetables and beans in a container; add the oil, vinegar, garlic, and basil. Cover the container with a tight-fitting lid. Refrigerate. Rotate the container from time to time to evenly coat the vegetables.

Makes about 2 1/2 cups

Orange Rice and Black Bean Salad

PREPARATION TIME: 6 minutes

Here is a way to turn cooked rice and canned black beans into a light, elegant meal.

1/2 cup canned black beans, drained
3/4 cup cooked brown rice
1/2 cup finely chopped celery (about 1 stalk)
1/2 cup peeled and sliced orange (1 small or 1/2 large)
1 scallion, thinly sliced (about 1/4 cup)
1 tablespoon chopped fresh cilantro
Salt and pepper

Dressing
1/4 cup orange juice
1 tablespoon cider or balsamic vinegar
1/2 teaspoon olive oil
1/2 teaspoon ground cinnamon

1. In a medium bowl, combine the beans, rice, celery, orange, scallion, and cilantro.
2. In a small bowl, combine the orange juice, vinegar, oil, and cinnamon.
3. Pour the dressing over the rice salad and stir thoroughly. Season with salt and pepper.

Makes one serving

White Bean
and Tomato Salad

PREPARATION TIME: 6 minutes

A rustic salad full of traditional flavor. The white beans give this salad a creamy, satisfying taste.

1 (15-ounce) can white beans
2 scallions, finely chopped
1 clove garlic, minced
1 celery stalk, thinly sliced
1 medium tomato, chopped
1 tablespoon fresh lemon juice
1/4 teaspoon dried basil
1/2 teaspoon olive oil
Salt and pepper
Pinch of red pepper flakes (optional)

1. Rinse the beans gently in a colander. Drain.
2. In a medium bowl, combine the beans, scallions, garlic, celery, tomato, lemon juice, basil, and olive oil. Gently mix.
3. Salt and pepper to taste. Sprinkle with red pepper flakes if you desire.

Makes two servings

Pineapple Banana Yogurt

PREPARATION TIME: **4 minutes**

For the best flavor, use a well-ripened banana with brown "sugar" flecks on the skin.

1 small banana, peeled and sliced
1/2 cup canned pineapple chunks, drained
1 cup vanilla yogurt

Extras (Optional)
Sliced orange segments
Chopped nuts
Granola

Peel and slice banana. In a medium bowl, combine banana, pineapple, and yogurt. Add your choice of extras.

Makes one serving

Taco Salad

PREPARATION TIME: 8 minutes

COOKING TIME: 5 minutes

If you don't feel like washing lettuce, make the salad anyway and forget the greens. This salad is too good to miss. Don't let the long ingredient list scare you—the salad takes only minutes to prepare.

1 teaspoon vegetable oil
1 cup frozen corn
1 tablespoon water
1 teaspoon ground cumin
1 medium avocado
1 tablespoon lemon or lime juice
1/2 medium tomato, chopped
2 tablespoons chopped scallion (about 1 scallion with the
    green part)
2 cups salad greens, torn into bite-size pieces
Salt
Baked tortilla chips, crumbled
1 tablespoon chopped fresh cilantro
Tabasco (optional)

1. In a small saucepan combine the oil, corn, water, and cumin. Cover and cook on medium heat for 3 minutes. Uncover and cook for 1 or 2 minutes to evaporate the excess moisture. Set aside.
2. Slice the avocado in half lengthwise. Remove the seed. Cut lengthwise and crosswise slices in the flesh making a grid pattern. Scoop the avocado cubes out of the shells and into a medium bowl. Gently stir in the lemon juice. Add the corn mixture, tomato, and scallion.

3. Spoon the salad onto a bed of greens. Salt to taste. Crumble a handful of baked tortilla chips and sprinkle them on top of the salad. Toss on the cilantro and a shake of Tabasco if desired. Serve and enjoy!

Makes two servings

Savory Downtown Salad

PREPARATION TIME: 7 minutes

This salad couldn't be simpler.

Choose any of the following:
Romaine or Boston lettuce,
      washed, dried, and torn into bite-size pieces
Slivered red or green cabbage slices
Fresh spinach
Avocado slices
Tomato slices
Shredded carrots
Sliced cooked beets
Bell pepper slices
Sliced celery
Sliced radishes
Sliced fresh mushrooms
Quartered artichoke hearts
Sliced cooked asparagus
Snow peas
Sliced scallion or red onion rings
Sliced cucumbers

Frozen green peas, thawed
Cooked garbanzo, kidney, or white beans
Toasted nuts
Sautéed tofu
Sunflower seeds
Croutons
Grated cheese
Chopped fresh parsley
Minced fresh basil

Select your favorite ingredients from the list, and compose a salad on a big plate. Pour on your favorite dressing and dig in.

Make as much or little as you like

Avocado and Pear Salad

PREPARATION TIME: 6 minutes

This simple green salad makes a light meal served with a slice of multigrain bread.

Romaine lettuce (4 large leaves or 3 to 4 lightly filled cups)
1 ripe avocado
1 medium-ripe pear, cored, peeled, and diced
1 tablespoon fresh lemon juice
Salt

1. Wash and dry the lettuce. Tear it into bite-size pieces, and pile the lettuce onto individual plates.

2. Slice the avocado in half lengthwise, and gently twist to remove the seed. Make lengthwise and crosswise cuts into the flesh every 1/2 inch. Scoop the avocado cubes out of the shells. Place the avocado and pear in a medium bowl. Sprinkle with the lemon juice and gently stir.

3. Mound the pear and avocado mixture onto the lettuce leaves. Salt to taste.

Makes two servings

Salad Dressing with Savoir Faire

Many good bottled salad dressings are on the market. If you have the time, make your own— but don't think salad dressing is any old vegetable oil and a $1.25 bottle of vinegar. To make a salad worth eating, you absolutely need to have a good dressing. Choose quality oil such as extra-virgin olive oil. A good vinegar is also essential; balsamic vinegar, mellow wine vinegar, or mild rice vinegar are good choices. Pick balsamic vinegar carefully and try different brands. There can be a big difference in flavor between the taste of pricey brands and budget brands.

The Basics

For foolproof dressing, add a little salt and garlic to your basic oil and vinegar. Some people like a sweetener in the dressing: Honey always works (just don't overdo it), and the taste of pure maple syrup will amaze you.

Dried herbs are fine for cooked food, but they are not strong enough for dressings (unless the dressing sits at least several hours). With a little extra cost and effort, you can make dressing sublime with fresh herbs. You can't go wrong with basil. Other good flavors include the tart sweetness of lemon, orange, and berry juices, or a sharp hint of mustard or horseradish. If you love creamy dressing, add a small amount of lowfat soft cheese, pureed silken tofu, or nonfat plain yogurt. Dressings will keep at least a week in the refrigerator in a tightly sealed container or jar, and the taste improves as the flavors merge.

Bright Lemon Vinaigrette

PREPARATION TIME: 5 minutes

This fresh dressing is lovely on lettuce salads. If you like, add a shake of Parmesan cheese when you toss the salad.

1/2 teaspoon lemon zest (paper-thin strips of the lemon skin)
3 tablespoons fresh lemon juice (about one medium lemon)
1/4 teaspoon salt
1 clove garlic, finely chopped
5 tablespoons olive oil

In a cup or small bowl, combine everything but the oil. Next, add the oil and whisk it in with a fork. Store in a covered jar in the refrigerator; it will keep for about 2 weeks.

Makes about 1/4 cup

Honey-Yogurt Dressing

PREPARATION TIME: 3 minutes

Use this sweet, creamy dressing on fruit salads.

1/3 cup plain yogurt
1 teaspoon honey
1/8 teaspoon vanilla
2 teaspoons orange juice concentrate (optional)

Combine the ingredients in a small bowl. If tightly covered and refrigerated, it will keep for about a week.

Makes about 1/2 cup

Creamy Garlic Dressing

PREPARATION TIME: 3 minutes

This dressing is delicious on lettuce salads, and it is also a tasty topping for baked or steamed potatoes.

1/2 cup plain yogurt
1 teaspoon Dijon mustard
2 cloves garlic, peeled and finely chopped
2 scallions, finely chopped
Salt and pepper

Whisk together the ingredients in a small bowl. If tightly covered and refrigerated, it will keep for about a week.

Makes about 1/2 cup

Sweet Mustard
Vinaigrette

PREPARATION TIME: 3 minutes

This mildly sweet dressing is luscious on a winter or spring salad with lettuce and citrus.

2 tablespoons cider vinegar
2 tablespoons Dijon mustard
2 tablespoons maple syrup or honey
1/3 cup olive oil
Salt

In a small bowl, whisk together the vinegar and mustard. Continue stirring while drizzling in the maple syrup and then the oil, until well blended. Add salt to taste. If tightly covered and refrigerated, it will keep at least 2 weeks.

Makes about 2/3 cup

CHAPTER 7

Fast Foods, Vegetarian-Style

Sandwiches, Tortilla Wraps, Sushi Rolls, and Pizzas

Sandwiches are a reliable mainstay for quick meals, and broadly defined, you'll find them popping up from around the globe in a variety of forms. Enjoy a warm Middle Eastern falafel sandwich tucked into Greek pita bread, a Baked Eggplant Sandwich on crusty sourdough, or a Grilled Sandwich with Onions and Mushrooms. Make a creamy Green Chile Quesadilla on a crisp Mexican corn tortilla, or a versatile Italian pizza, or delight in one-bite sushi snacks.

Garden Variety Sandwich

PREPARATION TIME: 7 minutes

Combine these simple ingredients any time of the day, and you'll have a fantastic meal.

Crusty whole grain bread

Filling
Choose any of the following:
A leaf or two of fresh basil
Arugula
Avocado slices
Cucumber slices
Green pepper rings
Lettuce
Mustard
Olive slices
Pickles
Pickled peppers
Radish slices
Red onion rings
Roasted red pepper slices
Seasoned tofu
Tomato slices

Place two slices of bread on the work surface, and brush each slice lightly with mustard. Pile any of your favorite fillings on one of the slices, and top the sandwich with the second slice of bread. Enjoy.

Makes one serving

Absent Egg Salad Sandwich

Preparation Time: 6 minutes

The texture of cubed Japanese-style silken tofu is very similar to that of boiled egg white in this sandwich. Spread the filling on toasted cracked-wheat bread. Tuck in a lettuce leaf or nutty-tasting arugula, and serve with juicy orange or tangerine slices.

3/4 cup Japanese silken firm tofu (about 6 ounces)
1/2 teaspoon fresh lemon juice
1 teaspoon prepared yellow mustard
1/2 teaspoon honey
1/4 teaspoon turmeric
1 tablespoon celery, diced
1 tablespoon onion, diced
1 teaspoon parsley, chopped
Dash of paprika
Salt and pepper to taste

Crumble the tofu in a mixing bowl with a fork. Add all of the remaining ingredients and stir to combine. Taste. If necessary add more salt and pepper. Refrigerated, it will keep for 2 or 3 days.

Makes two to three servings

Grilled Sandwich with Onion and Mushrooms

PREPARATION TIME: 15 minutes

A mushroom doesn't need to be psychedelic to expand your aware-ness. Pick your favorite whole grain bread or slices of crusty sour-dough, and make the ultimate grilled sandwich. Add a crisp salad and a sliced apple, and you have a delicious lunch or dinner. This sandwich is too good to miss!

1/4 pound mushrooms, thinly sliced (about 3 cups)
1 tablespoon olive oil
1/2 medium onion, thinly sliced
1/4 teaspoon salt
Pepper
2 teaspoons chopped parsley
4 slices bread (whole grain or sourdough)
Dijon mustard
Cheese: mozzarella, Fontina, or Jack (optional)
Butter, softened

1. Gently dust off any soil that clings to the mushroom with a soft paper towel. (Do not wash the mushrooms.)

2. Heat 1/2 tablespoon of olive oil in a medium nonstick skil-let. Add the onion and sauté over medium heat for about 5 minutes, until soft. Transfer to a bowl.

3. Heat the remaining oil in the skillet, add the mushrooms, salt, and a few pinches of pepper. Sauté the mushrooms over medium-high heat until golden and a little crisp on the edges, 5 to 6 minutes. Add 1/4 teaspoon water to the pan

to loosen the pan juices; stir for a moment. Add the mushrooms to the onions and stir together with the parsley.

4. Spread each slice of bread lightly with mustard. Pile the mushrooms and onions on two of the slices. Press the other two slices of bread on top of each sandwich. Lightly spread the top with butter. Place the sandwiches buttered side down on the skillet, and lightly spread the top side with butter. Cook over medium heat until golden, about 4 minutes, then turn and cook the underside. Serve immediately. Lean over your plate and take a juicy bite.

NOTE: If you desire, replace butter with olive oil. Lightly coat the pan with the oil.

Makes two servings

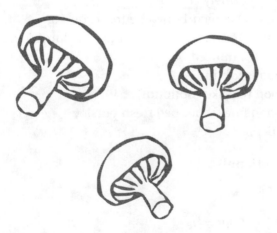

Falafel

Falafel is a spicy Middle Eastern pancake made from garbanzo beans. You can buy ready-made falafel mixes, but their taste or texture doesn't compare with falafel made from scratch. Stuff falafel into warm pocket bread with lettuce, tomato, and Tsiziki Sauce (page 43), a garlicky yogurt dressing. Here is a simple recipe for making these sumptuous pancakes without a mix. If there are extras, they won't last long. You don't need a food processor for this recipe—a masher or fork works fine.

$1/2$ medium red potato
2 teaspoons vegetable oil
1 small onion, finely chopped
1 ($15^{1}/2$-ounce) can garbanzo beans, drained
3 tablespoons fresh lemon juice (about $1/2$ large lemon)
2 cloves garlic, minced
2 tablespoons tahini
$1/2$ teaspoon paprika (optional)
1 tablespoon finely chopped fresh parsley
Salt and pepper

Extras (Optional)
Lettuce
Tomato
Tsiziki Sauce (page 43)

Preheat the oven to 350 degrees F.

1. Cut the potato into 1-inch chunks. Place the potato in a small saucepan with enough water to cover; boil until it is

tender, about 10 minutes. Drain. While the potato cooks, heat the oil in a small skillet over medium or medium-low heat and slowly sauté the onion until it is soft, stirring frequently, 8 to 10 minutes.

3. In a medium bowl, mash the potato, garbanzo beans, and lemon juice. Add the onion, garlic, tahini, paprika, if using, parsley, and salt and pepper to taste; stir to combine. The mixture will have a consistency similar to cookie dough.

3. Lightly oil a baking sheet with vegetable oil. Spoon the mixture onto the baking sheet, forming 3-inch pancakes. Place in the oven and bake for 15 minutes. Serve the falafel in a warm pocket bread, garnished if you like with lettuce, tomato, and Tsiziki Sauce. Yum!

Makes six servings; 12 (3-inch) pancakes

Broiled Zucchini Parmesan

PREPARATION TIME: 10 minutes

What you see is what you get in this open-face sandwich.

2 teaspoons olive oil
1/4 cup minced onion
1 clove garlic, minced
1 cup grated or thinly sliced zucchini
1/4 teaspoon dried basil
1/4 teaspoon dried oregano
4 tomato slices
2 slices multigrain bread
1 tablespoon grated Parmesan cheese
Pepper

1. Heat the oil in a medium skillet over medium heat. Sauté the onion and garlic until the onion is soft, about 3 minutes. Add the zucchini, basil, and oregano and continue cooking until it softens, about 3 minutes.

2. Layer half of the vegetables and tomato slices on each slice of bread. Lightly sprinkle with Parmesan cheese.

3. Broil for 1 minute or until the cheese melts. Pepper to taste. Eat with a knife and fork.

Makes one serving

Curry in a Hurry

PREPARATION TIME: 10 minutes

This recipe makes enough filling for two pocket halves. Corn, sweet peppers, and curry deliver a delicious warm flavor.

1 teaspoon olive oil
1/4 cup chopped scallion (about 2 scallions)
1/4 cup thinly sliced green bell pepper
1/4 teaspoon curry powder
1/3 cup frozen corn
1/2 medium tomato, chopped
Salt and pepper
1 pocket bread, cut in half

1. Heat the oil in a small skillet on medium heat, and sauté the scallion and bell pepper for about 2 minutes. Stir in the curry, corn, and tomato and cook for 3 to 5 minutes, stirring. Remove from the heat; salt and pepper to taste.

2. Scoop the filling inside the warm pocket bread.

Makes two servings

Baked Eggplant Sandwich

PREPARATION TIME: 6 minutes

COOKING TIME: About 20 minutes

Filling, fast, and oh, so delicious—everything you could want in a sandwich.

4 1/2-inch eggplant rounds
2 teaspoons olive oil
Salt and pepper
2 teaspoons balsamic or red wine vinegar
4 slices bread, sourdough or whole grain
Dijon mustard or pesto
4 tomato slices
2 to 3 thinly sliced onion rounds
2 slices Monterey Jack or Fontina cheese
Softened butter or olive oil
Dijon mustard or pesto

Preheat oven to 350 degrees F.

1. Wash the eggplant and cut away any blemishes you find on the skin. Slice off four half-inch rounds. (This is enough to make two sandwiches.) Rub the eggplant rounds with olive oil, and sprinkle with salt and a pinch of pepper. Lay eggplant on oiled baking sheet, and bake for 15 to 20 minutes, or until the eggplant is soft. Remove from the oven, and rub each slice with a few drops of vinegar.

2. Spread the bread thinly with Dijon mustard or pesto. Pile the eggplant, tomato, onions, and cheese onto two slices of bread. Top each sandwich with a second slice of bread.

Spread soft butter on the top of each sandwich. Place buttered side down in a skillet on medium-high heat. Spread the tops of the sandwich thinly with butter. Cook until the underside is golden. Turn and cook the other side. Serve immediately.

NOTE: The eggplant skin is edible. Be careful when you slice the eggplant because the skin is slick, and the knife can slip. If you do not want to eat the skin, peel the eggplant before slicing. Cooked eggplant will keep covered in the refrigerator for 2 to 3 days. If you like mild, sweet-tasting onions, sauté them for 5 minutes in the skillet in a teaspoon of oil before you grill the sandwich.

Makes one or two servings

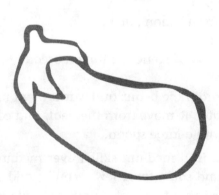

Crostini with a Bean
and a Green

PREPARATION TIME: 15 minutes

Italian crostini, literally "toast," is best made with crusty Italian or French bread, but any toasted bread will work. This version of crostini is covered with a creamy white bean spread mixed with greens.

1 (16-ounce) can white beans (1½ cups)
2 tablespoons water
2 teaspoons olive oil
1 large clove garlic, minced
2½ cups washed, tightly packed kale leaves without stems, finely chopped
2 tablespoons fresh lemon juice
Salt and pepper
3 or 4 slices of toasted French or Italian bread

1. Wash and drain the beans and warm them in a saucepan with the water. Remove from the heat, and coarsely mash the beans with a large spoon.

2. Heat the oil in a medium skillet over medium heat. Add the garlic and sauté for a few seconds; add the kale and stir. Cook, stirring frequently until the kale is tender and bright green, 7 to 10 minutes. The water that clings to the kale from washing is usually sufficient moisture for cooking. If the kale appears to be too dry, add water to the skillet 1 tablespoon at a time as necessary and continue sautéing.

3. When the kale is done cooking, add it, along with the lemon juice, salt, and pepper to the beans. Stir and taste. Add more salt and pepper if necessary. Spread the bean mixture onto the warm toasted bread for an open-faced sandwich, or use the toasted bread like you would chips, and eat the spread as a dip.

NOTE: If you like the sharp taste of uncooked garlic, add it to the beans when you add the lemon juice.

Makes two to three servings

Broiled Tofu

PREPARATION TIME: 5 minutes

TOFU PRESSING TIME: 30 minutes

COOKING TIME: About 10 minutes

Straight out of the box, tofu is a lot like pizza without a topping. But with a little planning, tofu might become your favorite fast food. Pressed tofu broils beautifully and tastes delicious. Pile broiled tofu onto a sandwich with your favorite toppings: mustard, relish, sliced onion, catsup, tomatoes, and crisp greens. It's so good you may find you've eaten it before there's time to build a sandwich. Make your own marinade or use hoisin sauce (available in well-stocked supermarkets and Asian markets). While the tofu is pressing, you'll have time to do a load of laundry.

1 block extra-firm or firm Chinese tofu (packaged in
    tubs of water)

Marinade
3 tablespoons balsamic vinegar
3 tablespoons soy sauce
2 teaspoons catsup

1. To press the tofu, sandwich the tofu between two plates. Weight the top plate with a heavy book, and let sit for 30 minutes. Remove the weight and top plate, and empty the water from the bottom plate. The tofu is now ready.

2. Preheat the broiler. Slice the pressed tofu into thirds, lengthwise. Place the tofu on a lightly oiled baking sheet and spread the tofu with the marinade.

3. Broil the tofu 3 to 4 inches from the heat for 5 to 7 minutes on each side, until browned and crisp on the edges. Serve it straight from the oven, or make a tofu sandwich on toasted multigrain bread topped with your favorite condiments.

Note: Prepared hoisin sauce can be substituted for the marinade.

Makes two servings

Pita with
Creamy Zucchini

PREPARATION TIME: 7 minutes

COOKING TIME: 5 minutes

Here is a simple shredded zucchini sandwich lightly flavored with yogurt and a hint of mint. Shredded vegetables have a wonderful texture and are great on top of pizza, inside tacos, or simply eaten straight from the pan. This version is tucked into a pita bread pocket.

1 medium zucchini
1 teaspoon olive oil
1 large clove garlic, minced
1/4 teaspoon dried mint
1/2 teaspoon dried oregano
1 tablespoon plain nonfat yogurt
Salt and pepper
1 whole wheat pita bread, cut in half

1. Shred the zucchini on the coarse side of a handheld grater with the largest holes.

2. In a medium skillet, heat the oil over medium heat. Sauté the zucchini, garlic, mint, and oregano, stirring often, until the zucchini is firm-tender and bright green, about 5 minutes.

3. Remove from the heat; stir in the yogurt. Season with salt and pepper. Scoop the filling into the warm pita bread halves. Mmm . . . this is a satisfying meal!

Makes one serving

Garlic Bread
with Attitude

PREPARATION TIME: 3 minutes

This method uses raw garlic, so the flavor will be sharp and biting.

1 or 2 slices bread
Olive oil
1 clove garlic, peeled

Preheat the broiler.

1. Lightly brush or drizzle the bread with olive oil and toast it under a broiler 3 to 4 inches from the heat. (It is good without the oil, too.) Watch closely because the bread will brown quickly.

2. Rub the toasted bread with the peeled garlic.

Makes one serving

Tortilla Wraps

Before you toss a package of tortillas into your shopping cart, read the nutrition label, because the ingredients vary greatly from brand to brand. The list for corn tortillas should be short: corn, lime, and water. Check out the number of fat grams on flour tortillas, and choose tortillas with the smallest number. (Some have zero fat, but their texture can be rubbery.) Also, look for refrigerated whole wheat tortillas free of preservatives. If you live in a community where freshly made tortillas are available, buy them—they're heavenly. Store all tortillas in the refrigerator or freezer. If you freeze them to use one at a time, let the tortilla thaw for a few minutes before cooking. Then, when the tortilla is warmed, it will toast and become crispy rather than steam and turn soggy. You can heat corn tortillas in a hot skillet with or without oil.

Green Chile Quesadilla

This quesadilla is delicious warmed on a dry skillet, but if you like the flavor of oil on your tortilla, add 1/4 teaspoon olive oil to the skillet before you warm it.

1/4 cup vegetarian canned refried beans
2 tablespoons canned, diced mild green chiles
2 (6-inch or 8-inch) wheat or corn tortillas
1/4 cup grated mozzarella cheese
1 tablespoon finely chopped fresh cilantro
Prepared salsa

1. Spread half of the beans and chiles on one half of each tortilla. Sprinkle the cheese and cilantro onto the filling.

2. Warm a dry skillet on medium heat. Heat each tortilla in the skillet. When the tortilla becomes pliable, fold the plain half of the tortilla over the filling and cook each side for about 2 minutes, or until the cheese melts.

3. Serve with prepared salsa.

Makes one serving (2 quesadillas)

Black Bean and
Yam Quesadilla

PREPARATION TIME: 20 minutes

Black beans and yams combine for striking flavor and color in this hearty tortilla wrap.

1 teaspoon vegetable oil
1/2 cup finely chopped onion (about 1/2 medium)
1 clove garlic, finely chopped
1 teaspoon ground cumin
2 teaspoons water
1 cup peeled grated yam (about 1/2 medium)
1/4 cup black beans, rinsed and drained
Salt and pepper
2 (8-inch or 10-inch) corn or wheat tortillas
1/4 cup grated Monterey Jack or mozzarella cheese
Prepared salsa

1. Heat the oil in a medium skillet over medium heat. Add the onion and garlic and sauté for 3 minutes or until the onion is soft. Add the cumin and water, and continue to sauté for 1 minute, stirring. Add the yam and beans, stir; cover and cook for about 6 minutes or until the yam is tender but not mushy.

2. Remove the skillet from the heat. Season the dish with salt and pepper, and put the yam mixture in a small bowl. In a minute or two, when the skillet is cool enough to handle, wipe it clean with a paper towel.

3. Place the quesadilla in the skillet on medium heat. Spoon on half of the yam mixture and sprinkle with half of the cheese. Cook the tortilla for about 30 seconds to soften, and then fold the tortilla in half and cook each side for about 2 minutes, until the cheese melts and the filling is warm. Repeat the process to make the second quesadilla. Serve with prepared salsa.

Makes one serving (2 quesadillas)

Tacos Monterrey

PREPARATION TIME: 10 minutes

COOKING TIME: 15 minutes

The distinctive smoky flavor in these unusual tacos comes from chipotle chiles. These chiles are tasty and very hot. You'll find small cans of chipotle chiles packed in adobo sauce in the Mexican section of the supermarket. (Mashed potatoes in a warm tortilla are delicious even without chipotle chiles. Add grated cheese and salsa to your taco instead.)

2 cups red or white potatoes, cut into 1/2-inch pieces
    (about 2 medium potatoes)
1/4 cup soy milk or dairy milk
1 canned chipotle chile, finely chopped
Salt
4 (6-inch) corn tortillas
1 teaspoon vegetable oil

1. Place the potatoes in a saucepan with enough water to cover; boil until tender, 10 to 15 minutes. Drain. Pour in the milk and mash the potatoes with a strong fork or masher until they are smooth and creamy. Add more milk if necessary. Stir in the chipotle chile. Taste. If you like food really hot, add one more chopped chipotle. Season with salt to taste.

2. Heat a tortilla on a hot, lightly oiled skillet over medium heat. The tortilla should be lightly toasted and flexible. Remove the tortilla from the skillet, and spread about 1/4 cup of the potato mixture down the center. Fold the tortilla around

the filling, and take a bite. Add more oil to the skillet if necessary, and cook the remaining tortillas.

Note: Freeze the remaining chipotle chiles for future meals. Spread the chiles out on a dinner plate so that they do not touch each other. Place the plate in the freezer for about 30 minutes. Next, put the frozen chiles into a plastic container, and store the container in the freezer. Now it will be easy to use the chiles one or two at a time.

Makes two servings

Spicy Zucchini Quesadilla

PREPARATION TIME: 8 minutes

Using jalapeño chiles is an inexpensive culinary trick that adds bright flavor to cooking. A little pepper costs about $0.05.

1 teaspoon olive oil
1/2 medium zucchini, thinly sliced (about 1 cup)
1/2 jalapeño chile (about 2 inches long), seeded, deveined, and finely chopped
2 (8-inch or 10-inch) wheat or corn tortillas
1 tomato (4 to 6 thin slices)
1 tablespoon chopped fresh cilantro or parsley
Grated mozzarella cheese, Monterey Jack, or feta cheese
    (1 to 2 tablespoons per quesadilla)
Prepared salsa

1. Heat the oil in a medium skillet on medium heat. Add the zucchini and jalapeño; sauté until the zucchini is tender, about 5 minutes. Stir occasionally.

2. Layer the zucchini mixture on one half of each tortilla. Add the tomato slices, cilantro, and cheese on top of the zucchini. When the skillet is cool enough to handle, wipe it with a paper towel. Reheat the skillet on medium heat. Place the quesadilla in the skillet, and when the tortilla becomes pliable, fold the plain half of the tortilla over the filling. Cook each side for about 2 minutes or until the cheese melts and the filling is hot. Cook the remaining quesadilla. Before you take a big bite, add salsa.

Makes one serving (2 quesadillas)

Taco Mania

PREPARATION TIME: 6 minutes

Expand your taco horizon with a one-pan meal teaming with tasty tidbits.

1 (8-inch or 10-inch) corn tortilla

Filling
Choose any of the following:
Chopped fresh tomato
Fresh lettuce, torn into bite-size pieces
Sliced avocado
Cooked brown rice
Sliced olives
Chopped onions or scallions
Grated cheese: Monterey Jack, Cheddar
Plain yogurt
Chopped fresh cilantro
Chopped green bell peppers
Diced canned mild green chiles
Leftover sweet potato
Warm refried beans
Salsa

Heat a tortilla on a hot dry skillet; when it's pliable, in about 30 seconds, fold the shell in half. Lightly toast both sides and remove from the heat. Stuff the tortilla with your favorite fillings.

Makes one serving

Hot Lips Fajita

PREPARATION TIME: 10 minutes

Fold a warm tortilla around sizzling sautéed vegetables, and you have a fabulous fajita. Jalapeño chiles fire up this version.

2 teaspoons vegetable oil
1 medium zucchini, thinly sliced (about 1 cup)
1/2 cup broccoli (about 6 florets)
1/4 cup chopped and seeded red bell pepper
    (about 1/4 pepper)
1/2 jalapeño chile, seeded and minced (about 2 inches long)
1/4 cup corn kernels (frozen or fresh)
1/4 teaspoon ground cumin
2 (10-inch) flour tortillas
1/4 cup shredded Monterey Jack or soy cheese

1. Heat the oil in a medium skillet over medium heat. Add all of the ingredients except the tortillas and cheese. Sauté the vegetables and cumin for 2 to 3 minutes, until the vegetables begin to soften and are crisp-tender.

2. Spoon half of the vegetable mixture and half the cheese onto a warm tortilla. Sprinkle with chopped red onion if you desire. Fold up one edge of the tortilla and wrap the other sides of the tortilla around the vegetables and cheese. Take a bite from the open end. There is enough filling to make a second serving.

NOTE: Heat the tortilla in a warm skillet, or roll it up in a damp paper towel, and heat it in a microwave for 25 seconds on High.

Makes two servings

Sushi

There is nothing difficult about making sushi. It's a great snack, and once the rice is cooked, it takes less time to prepare than a taco or burrito. Sushi has three essential ingredients: sheets of edible seaweed (nori), rice, and various fillings.

Making sushi at home is *far less* expensive than eating at a sushi bar or buying ready-made packages. A tray of eight from a deli costs nearly $5.00 (about $0.63 each). A tray of eight made in your kitchen costs a total of $0.45 (about $0.06 each). Add a crisp green salad on the side, a cup of hot tea or cold Japanese beer, and celebrate.

Sushi-Making Tips

- Short-grain white sushi rice is much easier to work with because it's stickier than other rice. You'll find sushi rice in the Asian section of a well-stocked supermarket or in Asian specialty shops. If you prefer brown rice, choose short-grain rice, as it's stickier than the long grain.

- Let the cooked rice cool to near room temperature before scraping it out of the pot. If the rice is cool, it's easier to get out of the pot and will be ready to use. Do not put hot rice on the nori, because it softens the sheet and makes rolling the sushi difficult.

- Sushi is traditionally rolled with a bamboo mat, called a *sudore*, but it's not an essential prop. It's easy to roll many forms of sushi without a mat. As you roll the sushi, gently press it as you proceed, being careful not to cause the filling to bulge along the roll, because the nori may tear.

- Moisten your fingers with water to keep the rice from sticking to them when you spread and lightly press the rice onto the nori sheet.

- Flavoring the rice: Some people like sushi rice plain. Most people prefer the rice dressed with a sweet rice-vinegar dressing. Buy prepared sushi rice vinegar that's ready to use, or make your own (see page 120).

Perfect Sushi Rice

PREPARATION TIME: 5 minutes

COOKING TIME (FOR WHITE RICE): 15 minutes

COOKING TIME (FOR BROWN RICE): 35 to 40 minutes

The following recipe makes enough rice to fill two 7 × 8-inch sheets of nori, and it makes about 16 bite-size pieces. Choose either white sushi rice or short-grain brown rice.

White rice
3/4 cup sushi rice
1 cup water

Brown rice
3/4 cup brown rice
1 1/2 cups water

In a pot with a lid, bring rice and water to a boil over the highest heat. As soon as steam escapes from below the lid, turn off the heat for 5 minutes. Return to low heat and simmer until water is absorbed, 10 to 15 minutes for white rice, or 35 to 40 minutes for brown rice. Do not stir the rice while it cooks or it will become gummy.

Makes 2 cups

Sushi Wheels

PREPARATION TIME: 10 minutes

Sushi Wheels filled with rice and bright-colored vegetables are worth making just for their visual appeal. They make excellent everyday snacks or carry-along meals.

2 cups cooked sushi rice, near room temperature, *not* hot
1 to 2 tablespoons sushi-rice vinegar or Sweet Sushi-Rice
    Dressing (page 120)
2 sheets nori (7 × 8 inches)

Filling
Choose your favorites from (about 1 cup total):
Carrot
Green onion
Cucumber
Avocado
Pickle
Red radish
Daikon radish
Scrambled egg
Tofu
Arugula
Parsley

1. Sprinkle rice with dressing and gently stir to combine.
2. Put the nori, shiny side down, on a flat work surface, with the long edge of the rectangle nearest you. Spread a thin layer of sushi rice (1/8- to 1/4-inch thick, about 1 cup) on the sheet of nori. The process is similar to spreading refried beans onto a taco shell, but here you do it with your fingers.

Moisten your fingertips with water first, and it will be easier. Leave a half-inch of exposed nori on the end of the sheet farthest away from you. You'll use this to seal the roll.

3. Place small pieces of the filling (about 4 tablespoons) on the rice, in a line about 1 1/2 inches from the edge nearest to you.

4. Carefully lift the edges of nori closest to you with both hands; gently fold the seaweed over the filling, capturing it in the first turn of the roll. Continue rolling away from you, gently pressing to create a well-shaped roll, like you were rolling up a sleeping bag. (Don't worry if a bit of rice and filling squeezes out of the two ends when you roll the sushi.)

5. When you're near the end of the nori, slightly moisten the exposed edge with water; continue rolling to the end of the sheet and lightly press to seal.

6. Place roll, seam side down, on the work surface. Cut into bite-size "wheels" (about 1-inch wide) with a sharp, wet knife. The first and last wheels on the roll may not be perfectly round or perfectly stuffed, but once you place them on a plate, cut side up, the problem disappears. Use soy sauce for dipping, if you wish.

NOTE: Sushi is usually filled with thinly sliced vegetables. For something different, try fruit-filled sushi. Choose among your favorites: apple, mango, kiwi, and pineapple. You want color and a bit of crunch. Have fun creating your own delightful masterpiece.

Makes 16 individual sushi wheels

Sweet Sushi-Rice Dressing

PREPARATION TIME: 3 minutes

Use about 1 tablespoon of dressing to flavor 1 cup of rice.

2 tablespoons rice vinegar or white vinegar
1 to 2 tablespoons sugar
Pinch of salt

Mix 2 tablespoons of vinegar with 1 tablespoon of sugar. Stir until the sugar dissolves. Taste. If you like, add more sugar.

Makes 2 tablepsoons, enough to flavor 2 cups rice

Pizza—There Are Many Paths to Pizza

Build pizza on a variety of foundations. Try English muffins, Italian focaccia, Boboli, bagels, French bread, or store-bought fresh or frozen pizza dough. Unless you love extra-thick pizza crust, cut Boboli bread in half to create two rounds of pizza, or buy thin-crust Boboli.

The following recipes are for mini-pizzas that use pita bread for the base. There is enough topping for two 6-inch pizzas. When you choose a larger pizza crust, increase the topping amounts.

Pita Pizza Crust

PREPARATION TIME: 3 minutes

Lightly toasted pita bread makes the perfect "crust" for a quick and easy pizza.

1 (6-inch) pita bread

Preheat the oven to 450 degrees F.

Lightly toast the pita bread for 3 minutes in the oven. Remove the pita from the oven. If you like thin-crust pizza, carefully split the pita bread around its outer edge to yield two equal rounds. If you like a thicker-crust pizza, use the pita whole.

Makes one or two 6-inch crusts

Pepper and
Mushroom Pizza

PREPARATION TIME: 12 minutes

This straightforward combination is the essence of pizza.

2 teaspoons olive oil
1/4 cup chopped onion
1/2 cup chopped bell pepper
1 1/2 cups sliced mushrooms (about 6)
1/4 teaspoon dried basil
1 (6-inch) pita bread
6 thin tomato slices
Grated mozzarella cheese

Preheat the oven to 450 degrees F.

1. Heat the oil in a small skillet over medium heat. Add the onion, bell pepper, mushrooms, and basil; sauté, stirring frequently for 3 minutes, or until the vegetables begin to soften. Remove from the heat.

2. Lightly toast the pita bread for 3 minutes in the oven. Remove the pita from the oven. Carefully split the pita bread around its outer edge to yield two equal rounds.

3. Spoon the filling onto the crust. Add tomato slices and lightly sprinkle with grated mozzarella cheese. Heat the pizza in the oven until the tomatoes are warm and the cheese begins to melt, about 2 minutes. Serve immediately.

Makes two servings

Vegan Farmhouse Pizza

PREPARATION TIME: 12 minutes

This gourmet pizza works without cheese.

2 teaspoons olive oil
1/4 cup diced onion
1/2 cup chopped apple
1 cup prewashed fresh spinach, tightly packed and then
    chopped
1 (6-inch) pita bread
1/2 teaspoon Dijon mustard
1 teaspoon chopped walnuts

Preheat the oven to 450 degrees F.

1. Heat the oil in a medium skillet on medium-high heat.
   Sauté the onion for 3 minutes. Add the apple and spinach;
   cook until the spinach wilts, 3 to 5 minutes. Press out excess moisture.

2. Lightly toast the pita in the oven for 3 minutes. Remove the
   pita from the oven and lower the heat to 350 degrees F. Carefully slice it in half around its outer edge to yield two equal
   rounds.

3. In a bowl, combine the spinach mixture and mustard.
   Spread the topping onto the toasted pita bread. Sprinkle with
   the walnuts, and warm in the oven for about 5 minutes.

Makes two servings

Roasted Vegetable Pizza

PREPARATION TIME: 7 minutes

COOKING TIME: 20 minutes

This pizza is full of luxurious flavor.

1 medium red potato, thinly sliced
1 small zucchini, cut into 1/4-inch slices (about 1 cup)
1/3 medium bell pepper, coarsely chopped
1/2 cup coarsely chopped onion
1 large clove garlic, minced
1 teaspoon olive oil
1/2 teaspoon dried thyme
1 (6-inch) pita bread
Grated Parmesan cheese (optional)

Preheat the oven to 425 degrees F.

1. Place the potato, zucchini, bell pepper, onion, and garlic in a medium bowl. Add the oil and thyme and stir to evenly coat the vegetables with oil. Spread the vegetable mixture onto a baking sheet. Don't crowd them or they'll steam, not roast. Bake for about 20 minutes or until the potatoes are tender. Stir once or twice to ensure even cooking. Remove from the oven. Raise the oven heat to 450 degrees F.

2. Lightly toast the pita bread for 3 minutes in the oven. Remove the pita from the oven. Carefully split the pita bread around its outer edge to yield two equal rounds.

3. Spoon the filling onto the crust. If you desire, sprinkle each pizza with 1 or 2 teaspoons of grated Parmesan cheese and heat in the oven just until the cheese begins to melt. Enjoy.

Makes two servings

Zucchini and Cheese Pizza

PREPARATION TIME: 10 minutes

Halved pita bread makes a thin crust for lightly sautéed slivers of zucchini sprinkled with basil.

1 teaspoon olive oil
1/4 cup finely chopped onion
1/4 teaspoon dried basil
1 small zucchini, grated (about 1 cup)
1/2 cup chopped tomato
1 (6-inch) pita bread
Grated Monterey Jack cheese
Salt and pepper

Preheat the oven to 450 degrees F.

1. Heat the oil in a medium skillet over medium heat. Sauté the onion and basil for 3 minutes. Add the zucchini and cook, stirring frequently, for 2 minutes. Add the tomato, and cook for another minute. Remove from the heat.

2. Lightly toast the pita bread for 3 minutes in the oven. Remove the pita from the oven. Carefully split the pita bread around its outer edge to yield two equal rounds.

3. Spoon the filling onto the two crusts. Sprinkle with grated Monterey Jack cheese. Return the pizza to the oven and bake just until the cheese melts, 1 or 2 minutes. Season with salt and pepper.

Makes two servings

Pizza Party

One of the best parts about making party-size pizza at home is that you're freed from trying to recycle the unwieldy cardboard box that never fits into the trash bin. Traditional ungarnished Italian pizza is made with a crust, tomato sauce, and melted cheese, but you can toss on just about anything that will withstand a 400–degree F heat. To cut the cost, consider a potluck party, and ask your friends to bring toppings.

Eight Pizza-Making Tips

1. My main advice about homemade pizza is to have fun.

2. Pizza dough likes to be warm. If you store your flour and oil in the refrigerator, make sure they're at room temperature before you begin.

3. Some toppings need precooking (see the list on page 131). Mushrooms, for example, can release a lot of liquid if they are put on raw, which can make your pizza soggy. Cook them first in a lightly oiled nonstick skillet on medium high until they are soft.

4. If you like a tiny bit of crunch to your pizza, add a teaspoon of cornmeal to the dough, or sprinkle a teaspoon of cornmeal on the pizza pan before putting on the dough.

5. Put the topping out to the very edge so there is no crust to discard. This makes the pizza seem bigger.

6. Garnish the pizza with fresh herbs after baking. If fresh herbs are put on before baking, flavor is lost in the oven.

7. If you use Parmesan cheese, sprinkle it on after you take the pizza out of the oven. You'll get more flavor that way.

8. If you don't have a pizza cutter, use a silverware knife, and save the edge of your chef's knife for cutting vegetables.

Pizza Dough

MIXING AND KNEADING TIME: 10 minutes

DOUGH RISING TIME: 25 minutes

COOKING TIME: 12 to 15 minutes

Don't let the fact that pizza is made from a yeast dough scare you. It's easy! You won't need a rolling pin to form this soft dough; shape it right in the pan with your hands. Enjoy!

1/2 cup whole wheat flour
1 tablespoon active dry baking yeast (1 1/2 packages)
1/4 teaspoon sugar or honey
1/2 teaspoon salt
1/2 cup warm water
2 tablespoons olive oil
1/2 to 5/8 cup unbleached white flour

Preheat oven to 500 degrees F.

1. In a medium mixing bowl, combine the whole wheat flour, yeast, sugar, and salt. Mix.

2. In a small saucepan, warm the water and oil. Remove from stove. When water feels warm to your hand, but not hot, add it to the flour mixture. Beat with a spoon until almost smooth and the dough is the consistency of pancake batter. Stir in 1/2 cup white flour.

3. Turn the dough onto a lightly floured surface, and gradually add white flour, 1/2 teaspoon at a time, until you have a smooth dough and it is no longer tacky or sticks to your hands. Knead for several minutes until smooth and elastic.

4. Oil the mixing bowl. Pat the dough into a ball and place it in the bowl, turning to coat with oil. Set it aside to rise for 25 minutes in a warm place while you prepare toppings. If you're not ready for the dough after it rises, punch it down, and let it rise again for another 20 to 25 minutes.

5. Place the dough in the center of a greased 12-inch to 14-inch pan and push and pat the dough toward the edge, forming a 12-inch circle. If any holes or tears appear, repair by pinching the dough together. (Pizza doesn't have to be round. Make a rectangle, square, or free form.)

6. Add your favorite toppings. Bake on the top shelf of a very hot oven, 500 degrees, for 12 to 15 minutes.

NOTE: Mix the dough with your hands. At first, it will stick to your fingers, but as you add the additional flour, a teaspoon at a time, the dough will form into a lump.

Makes one (12-inch) pizza

Topping It Off

Some people like their pizza piled high with many toppings; some like a simple pizza with a few flavors. Make pizza with or without tomato sauce. Spread the topping mixed like confetti, or put different vegetables on single sections or in stripes across the pizza dough. Adding intense flavors like garlic makes a pizza interesting.

Sauce Possibilities

Commercial pizza sauce
Commercial pasta sauce
4-ounce can of tomato sauce flavored with
   1 teaspoon oregano

Topping Possibilities

These toppings are ready to use without precooking.

Artichoke hearts (commercial, packed in water, drained)
Bell peppers, red or green
Capers
Garlic
Green chiles
Green onions (add after baking)
Olives
Onions, red or yellow
Pineapple
Red chili
Roasted red peppers
Sun-dried tomatoes (Pour boiling water over dry-packed
   tomatoes, soak for 5 minutes, drain.)
Tomatoes

More Topping Possibilities

Precook these vegetables. Season with salt and pepper and a squeeze of lemon if you desire. (Add them before you bake the pizza even though they are precooked.)

Asparagus   Snap off tough stem ends. Cut the spears in quarters. Simmer in water in a small saucepan until crisp-tender.

Broccoli   Cook in lightly oiled skillet on medium high heat until crisp-tender.

Eggplant   Slice into half-inch thick rounds, brush with oil, and bake at 350 degrees F until soft, or broil for 4 or 5 minutes on each side until lightly browned.

Mushrooms   Cook in lightly oiled skillet on medium high heat until soft.

Spinach   Sauté in lightly oiled skillet on medium high heat until soft.

Zucchini   Sauté in lightly oiled skillet on medium high heat until crisp-tender.

Cheese Possibilities

Cheddar	Monterey Jack
Feta	Mozzarella
Gouda	Parmesan

Herb Possibilities (fresh or dried)

Basil	Parsley (fresh)
Cilantro (fresh)	Rosemary
Oregano	

CHAPTER 8

Bean Meals

Beans are just about the perfect food. Eat them straight from the pot, wrapped in tortillas, tossed into soup, or made into dips. The quick route to eating beans is to buy them in cans. When you have time for soaking and simmering dried beans, a thrifty meal becomes dirt cheap.

Spilling the Beans—Gut Instincts

If you avoid eating beans because of fear of flatulence (gas), there's good news. Beans contain sugars that humans cannot digest. When these sugars arrive in the large intestine, bacteria ferment them, producing gas. When beans become part of your regular diet, however, the body adapts and the intestinal problem disappears.

People react differently to beans. If someone you know complains of discomfort after eating them, don't assume that will happen to you. If beans are new to your diet, eat them more frequently in small portions, and avoid mixing beans in the same meal with other gas-producing vegetables, such as cabbage. There are products on the market sold in natural food stores that help prevent the gas that beans cause. Beano is one brand name. Just add a few drops to your first bite.

Buying the Best Beans

Look for unbroken dried beans with a deep vibrant color, and store them in airtight containers in a cool, dry, dark place.

Bean Cooking Chart

1 cup Dried Beans	Water (cups)	Cooking Time	Yield (cups)
Black	4	2 hours	2
Black-eyed peas	3	1 hour	2
Garbanzo	4	3 hours	4
Great Northern	$3^1/_2$	2 hours	2
Kidney	3	$1^1/_2$ hours	2
Lentils	3	45 minutes	$2^1/_4$
Lima	3	$1^1/_2$ hours	$1^1/_4$
Navy	3	$2^1/_2$ hours	2
Pinto	3	$2^1/_2$ hours	2
Red	3	3 hours	2
Soy	4	$2^1/_2$ hours	3
Split peas	3	45 minutes	$2^1/_4$

Cooking Dried Beans

- Sort through dried beans. Pour the portion you are about to use onto a pan or dish. Run your fingers through them, and pick out any pebbles, twigs, or shriveled old beans you find. You will rarely find any, but it's worth looking. The last thing you want is a dentist's bill for a broken tooth from chomping on a rock. Pour the sorted beans into a colander and give them a quick rinse.

- Soak dried beans for 6 to 8 hours—overnight works well. Use plenty of water because beans swell during this process. (Lentils, split peas, and black-eyed peas do not need pre-soaking.)

- Drain the beans after soaking and they're ready to cook.

- Put the beans in a pot, and cover them with fresh water. Put a lid on the pot, and bring it to a boil. Then lower the heat and simmer until the beans are thoroughly cooked. Check periodically to see that the beans remain covered with water, and replenish if necessary.

Refried Pinto Beans

PREPARATION TIME: 15 minutes

Top this dish with salsa, add a side of rice, and you'll have a delicious, down-to-earth meal, or get out the chips and have a hearty snack. Of course they're great in tacos, too.

1^{1}/$_{2}$ cups cooked pinto beans or (15-ounce canned pinto beans, rinsed and drained)
1 to 3 tablespoons water (use more if necessary)
1 tablespoon olive oil
1/4 cup onion, minced (about 1/4 medium onion)
1 to 2 cloves garlic, minced
1^{1}/$_{2}$ teaspoons chili powder
1/2 teaspoon cumin powder
1/2 teaspoon dried oregano
2 tablespoons plain yogurt
2 tablespoons grated Cheddar or Monterey Jack cheese
1/4 teaspoon vinegar (apple cider vinegar or red wine vinegar)
Salt
2 tablespoons canned green chiles (optional)

1. In a medium bowl, mash the beans, adding as much water as necessary to make them creamy and thick; add a tablespoon of liquid at a time. Set mixture aside.

2. In a small skillet, heat oil on medium-high heat; add onion and cook for 2 to 3 minutes until the onion is translucent. Add garlic, chili powder, cumin, oregano, and stir. Continue cooking for another minute. Add the beans and cook for a minute or two over moderately low heat until warm. Stir in yogurt, cheese, and vinegar. Remove from heat and taste.

3. Adjust the seasoning, and salt to taste. Add more chili power if you like it hotter. Stir in chiles, if you desire.

NOTE: Mash the beans with a fork, spoon, or potato masher; the beans like to bounce around in the bowl when you begin, but once the skins break and you add a little water, it's easy.

Makes one or two servings

Chipotle–Black Bean Chili

PREPARATION TIME: 10 minutes

The chipotle chile pepper is the ingredient that gives this chili its deep flavor. You'll find chipotles in cans in the Mexican section of the supermarket. They come packed in adobo sauce, a very hot Mexican red sauce. A can of chipotle chiles goes a long way. It takes only 1 or 2 small chipotles to flavor a whole pot of chili.

1 teaspoon olive oil
1/2 cup chopped onion (about 1/2 small)
3 cloves garlic, minced
2 tablespoons chili powder
1 teaspoon minced canned chipotle pepper (1 chipotle)
2 (15-ounce) cans black beans, drained
2 (14 1/2-ounce) cans stewed whole tomatoes, undrained and
    chopped
1 (4 1/2-ounce) can chopped mild green chiles, drained
Salt and pepper

1. Heat the oil over medium heat in a large saucepan or skillet. Add the onion and garlic, and sauté 3 to 5 minutes until the onion is tender; stir frequently. Add the remaining ingredients. Bring to a boil.

2. Reduce the heat and simmer for 15 minutes. Ladle the chili into a bowl, and enjoy.

NOTE: Freeze remaining canned chipotle chiles for future meals.

Makes four servings

Chili Uno-Dos-Tres

PREPARATION TIME: 10 minutes

COOKING TIME: 35 minutes

This chili looks good and tastes great.

2 teaspoons olive oil
3/4 cup chopped onion (about 1 small)
3 cloves garlic, finely chopped
1/2 cup medium red or green bell pepper, diced
1 cup water
2 tablespoons chili powder
1 1/2 teaspoons ground cumin
1 (14 1/2-ounce) can ready-cut tomatoes, undrained
1 (15-ounce) can red kidney beans, drained
1 (15-ounce) can garbanzo beans, drained

1. Heat the oil in a medium skillet over medium heat. Add the onion, garlic, and bell pepper; sauté 5 to 7 minutes, stirring frequently.
2. Add the water, chili powder, cumin, tomatoes, kidney beans, and garbanzo beans. Bring to a boil. Reduce the heat; gently simmer, uncovered, for 30 minutes. Ladle into a bowl and serve with corn bread if you desire. ¡Olé!

Makes two or three servings

Black-Eyed Peas

PREPARATION TIME: 6 minutes

COOKING TIME: 45 to 55 minutes

Black-eyed peas are one of the few beans you can cook without pre-soaking. They cook in about 45 to 55 minutes and taste the same whether you soak them or not, but they won't look the same. When beans soak overnight, they slowly rehydrate and hold their shape throughout the cooking process. Without presoaking, a violent re-hydration occurs, causing some of the skins to crack and separate from the beans. (It sounds more murderous than it really is.) If you're using the beans in a salad, consider soaking them first to improve their appearance. If looks don't matter, start cooking.

If you're out of onion and bell pepper, cooked black-eyed peas can stand on their own dressed with fresh lemon juice and a splash of olive oil. If you're in the mood for a simple-to-prepare, delicious meal, forget the soaking and start cooking.

2 cups dried black-eyed peas
1 small onion, finely chopped (about 1 cup)
1 medium bell pepper, chopped (about 1 cup)
1 teaspoon dried oregano

Toppings
Olive oil
Fresh lemon juice
Salt and pepper
Chopped tomato
Fresh cilantro

1. Cover the beans with fresh water; add the onion, bell pepper, and oregano. Bring the pot to a boil, and simmer until the beans are tender, 45 to 55 minutes. Keep the pot partially covered at all times. Check the beans occasionally, and add more water if needed.

2. Remove the beans from the pot with a slotted spoon; dress them with a drizzle of olive oil, lemon juice, and salt and pepper to taste. If you're a garlic fanatic, mince some and toss it on, too.

3. Garnish with chopped tomato and cilantro.

NOTE: For variety, garnish the black-eyed peas with salsa, a splash of Tabasco, or Vietnamese chili sauce. Black-eyed peas are also delicious spooned over cooked rice or added to soups.

If you choose to presoak the beans, here's how to do it: Cover the beans with twice their volume of water, and soak for 8 hours or overnight. Drain.

Makes four servings

Dal

Cooking Time: About 30 minutes

This souplike dish made with lentils is the Indian version of a stew. It's a robust one-pot meal for any time of the day. Garnish a bowl of dal with sliced avocado, chopped fresh tomato, a dollop of yogurt, or a spoonful of chutney. Pour yourself a cup of hot tea, and add a plate of sliced pineapple or mango on the side.

1 cup dried lentils
3 cups water
2 cups finely chopped onion (about 2 medium)
2 teaspoons olive oil
2 cloves garlic, finely chopped
1 teaspoon curry powder
Salt

1. In a medium saucepan, combine the lentils, water, and 1 cup of onion. Bring the ingredients to a boil; reduce the heat, cover the pan, and simmer until the lentils are tender, about 30 minutes.

2. While the lentils are cooking, heat the oil in a medium skillet; add the remaining 1 cup onion, garlic, and curry. Sauté the vegetables on medium or medium-low heat, stirring occasionally until the onions are golden, soft, and just beginning to brown, 10 to 15 minutes.

3. Add the onion mixture to the cooked lentils, stirring to combine. Heat the lentil mixture for a few minutes longer. Salt to taste.

NOTE: You'll find lentils in the supermarket near the dried beans.

Makes four servings

Easy Pot-o-Chili

<small>PREPARATION TIME:</small> 15 minutes

<small>COOKING TIME:</small> 60 to 90 minutes

Cook up a pot of chili and call your friends for a fiesta. Soak the beans for 6 to 8 hours before you plan to cook them, and allow about 1 hour for the beans to simmer. Serve with a big slice of hot corn bread, and top the beans with salsa and a dollop of yogurt if you desire.

2 teaspoons vegetable oil
1 cup chopped onion (about 1 medium)
2 cloves garlic, finely chopped
1 cup dried beans, presoaked (small red beans or
    kidney beans)
1 (14-ounce) can diced tomatoes
2 tablespoons canned diced green chiles
1 tablespoon chili powder
1 teaspoon powdered cumin
1 tablespoon cornmeal
Salt

1. In a large pot, heat the oil and sauté the onion and garlic on medium to medium-low heat for 6 to 10 minutes or until tender.

2. Drain the beans. Add the beans to the pot with enough fresh water to cover. Bring the pot to a boil, and then reduce the heat to low. Cover and simmer until the beans are tender, about 60 minutes. Check the pot occasionally to see that the beans remain covered with water.

3. When the beans are tender, add the tomatoes, green chiles, chili powder, cumin, and cornmeal. Taste and then season with salt. Gently simmer for another 10 to 15 minutes uncovered, stirring occasionally.

NOTE: If you like really thick chili, add more cornmeal a tablespoon at a time.

Makes four servings

White Bean Jumble

Preparation Time: 12 minutes

Cooking Time: 15 minutes

This tasty combination satisfies a hearty appetite. Don't let kale's stiff-looking leaves put you off; cooked, they become soft and delicious.

2 large white or red potatoes
1 cup chopped firmly packed kale leaves, with stems removed
2 teaspoons olive oil
1/2 cup chopped onion (about 1/2 small)
1 clove garlic, chopped
1/2 teaspoon dried thyme
1 small tomato, chopped
1/2 cup canned white beans, rinsed and drained
Salt and pepper

1. Wash the potatoes and cut them into 1/2-inch bite-size pieces. Add an inch of water to a steamer pot with a steamer basket. Cover the pot, and bring the water to a boil. Add the potatoes and steam for about 10 minutes, or until the potatoes are barely tender.

2. While the potatoes steam, wash the kale and remove stems; run a knife along each side of the stem to free the leaf. Discard the stems. Gather the leaves into a pile, and hold them together with one hand while you cut the kale into about 1-inch slices. When the potatoes are done, remove the pot from the heat and uncover it. Set the potatoes aside.

3. Heat the oil in a medium skillet over medium heat. Add the onion, garlic, and thyme; sauté, stirring frequently for about 3 minutes or until the onion softens and becomes translucent. Add the kale and tomato, and sauté for 1 to 2 minutes, stirring until the kale has wilted. Add the potatoes and beans and heat for a minute or two. Salt and pepper to taste. Serve immediately.

Makes one or two servings

Pete's Harbor Special

Prepared in a matter of minutes, this uncomplicated meal is full of flavor. It's the Monday night menu special from a fisherman's cafe on the San Francisco Bay.

1 medium zucchini
2 teaspoons olive oil
$1/2$ teaspoon dried thyme
1 cup canned vegetarian refried beans
1 clove garlic, minced
Salt and pepper
Prepared salsa
Grated mozzarella or Monterey Jack cheese (optional)

1. Wash and dry the zucchini. Cut off the ends. Next, cut the zucchini diagonally into long, oval-shaped $1/4$-inch-thick slices.

2. Heat the oil in a medium skillet on medium-high heat. Add the zucchini and sprinkle with thyme. Quickly fry the zucchini slices until they are golden-speckled on both sides, about 10 minutes. Remove the zucchini from the pan.

3. Heat the beans and garlic in a small saucepan. Spread the beans in a thin layer onto a warm plate. Arrange the zucchini slices on the beans. Season with salt and pepper. Add a splash of salsa and a sprinkle of grated mozzarella or Monterey Jack cheese, if desired. (Place the plate in a warm oven on low heat for a minute or two to melt the cheese if you desire.)

Makes one serving

Black Bean Quickie

PREPARATION TIME: 6 minutes

Here is a hearty meal without cooking. Eat this dish as a dip with baked tortilla chips, or pile it onto crusty sourdough bread.

1 (15-ounce) can black beans, drained
1 avocado
1/2 cup prepared Mexican-style red salsa
1 to 2 tablespoons chopped fresh parsley or cilantro
1/2 chopped medium tomato
Salt and pepper

1. In a medium bowl, roughly mash the beans with a fork or masher.

2. Halve the avocado lengthwise and gently twist to separate it from the pit. Make lengthwise and crosswise cuts about 1/2 inch apart in the flesh of each half. Scoop the avocado cubes out of the skin, and add them to the beans. Stir in the salsa, parsley, and chopped tomato. Salt and pepper to taste.

3. Serve as a dip or use as a sandwich spread.

Makes about 2 cups

Marinated Tempeh

PREPARATION TIME: 15 minutes

Tempeh is a favorite Indonesian soy food made from fermented soy-beans. Think of it as tofu's sibling. It has a chunkier texture and a bit more flavor than tofu. Like tofu, tempeh acts as a sponge, soaking up the flavors that surround it. If you are still struggling with the idea of giving up meat, tempeh has a very "meaty" texture, and you can do anything to tempeh that you can do to meat. To keep tempeh fresh, store it in your refrigerator. It freezes well and keeps its flavor and texture for several months. You'll find tempeh widely available in natural food stores and even some supermarkets. If you notice a few dark spots on the tempeh when you open the package, that's normal. Eat this dish straight out of the frying pan or add it to soups, stews, salads, grains, chili, or filled tortillas.

2 ounces tempeh
1 tablespoon white or cider vinegar
1 tablespoon soy sauce
1 1/2 teaspoons water
1 large clove garlic, minced
1 teaspoon vegetable oil
Pepper

1. Cut the tempeh into about ¼-inch-thick strips or cubes and set aside. In a shallow bowl, stir together the vinegar, soy sauce, water, and garlic.

2. Add the tempeh and stir it around a few times. Let it sit in the marinade for a few minutes to absorb the sauce.

3. In a medium skillet, heat oil on medium-high heat, and sauté the tempeh for about 8 minutes until it is golden and crisp. If necessary, add a little more oil to prevent sticking. Pepper to taste, and serve immediately.

NOTE: Tempeh can be easily cooked by broiling. Marinate the tempeh following the recipe directions. Lightly oil a baking dish, and broil the slices 3 to 4 inches from heat for 3 to 5 minutes on each side until lightly browned.

Makes one serving

CHAPTER 9

Grain Meals

Whole grain cooking is one of the most enjoyable discoveries a new vegetarian can make. Marketers design the ads you see for quick-cooking grains and rice cookers to make you think there is something mysterious and difficult about cooking grains. You'll soon see that cooking whole grains is as simple as boiling water. There are only two things that can go wrong: too much water or too little water, and that's easy to fix. If the grain is not tender at the end of the cooking time, add more water—just a little, 1/4 cup or less—and let the grain cook a little longer. If you added too much water, lift the cooked grain out of the pot with a slotted spoon, leaving the excess water behind. The grain may be soggy, but you can use less water next time.

Store uncooked grains, especially cornmeal, in the refrigerator or freezer. It doesn't take long for hungry insects to find a warm kitchen and begin feasting on your food supply. They know a good thing when they find it.

The Perfect Pot—of Grain, of Course

Here's a selection of favorite grains that are part of vegetarian cuisine. Rice, wheat, corn, oats, and buckwheat feed most of the world.

Bulgur Basic bulgur, or cracked wheat, is a wonderfully easy grain to prepare. Measure 1 cup of bulgur into a heat-proof bowl, and pour in 1 cup of boiling water. Cover the bowl, and set it aside for about 20 minutes. When the bulgur has absorbed the water, stir to fluff the grains. If it's still too chewy, add more hot water. (One cup of dry bulgur yields 2$^1/_2$ cups cooked.)

Couscous Part of its celebrated reputation is due to the fact that it's quick to prepare. Place equal amounts of boiling water and dry couscous in a heat-proof bowl. Cover and let sit for about 10 minutes. Stir to fluff the grain. If it's still crunchy, add a small amount of hot water. (One cup of dry couscous yields 2$^1/_3$ cups cooked.)

Kasha or Buckwheat Groats This eastern European dish has been a staple food for centuries. You'll find kasha at natural food stores and in the kosher section of many supermarkets. If the kasha you buy is dark brown, it's already been roasted; but if it's pale in color, pan-roast $^1/_2$ cup briefly on medium heat in a dry skillet until it begins to change color to bring out its hearty flavor. Boil 1 cup of water with a pinch of salt, pepper, and a splash of oil. Pour the liquid into the skillet with the kasha, cover, and simmer on very low heat for 15 minutes. (Yields 1$^1/_4$ cups.)

Noodles One of the most popular quick-cooking grains of all. Boil a pot of water; add noodles; cook until al dente. Drain the noodles immediately. (Al dente means "to the tooth"—chewy but not mushy.)

Old-Fashioned Rolled Oats   A bowl of hot oatmeal is delicious any time of the day and takes about 10 minutes to prepare. Its taste and texture are far superior to instant or quick-cooking oats.

Stove-top cooking: In a pot with a tight-fitting lid, bring 1 cup of water, 1/2 cup of old-fashioned rolled oats, and 1/4 to 1/2 teaspoon salt to a boil; then lower the heat to medium-low and continue cooking, stirring frequently, for 5 to 7 minutes or until the oatmeal is thick and creamy. Remove from heat, and let it stand for a few minutes before serving. Makes 1 cup.

Microwave cooking: Combine 1/2 cup of old-fashioned rolled oats and 1 cup of water in a big microwavable bowl. You need a lot of room in the bowl because the oatmeal bubbles and spurts. Cover the bowl with a glass plate while it cooks to avoid a big cleanup. Microwave on Medium for 2 minutes, stir, and heat for 2 minutes more or until the oats have thickened. Mix well before serving. Makes 1 cup.

Polenta (Cornmeal)   One of the best ways imaginable to eat corn. Serve the polenta while it's soft and warm, or pour it into a baking pan or onto a plate and refrigerate it to eat later. As polenta cools, it becomes firm and ready for slicing. When you're ready to eat, cut the polenta into slices and heat it in a skillet, the oven, or the broiler. It will keep refrigerated for several days.

Determining the amount of water used in cooking polenta is not an exact science and can vary slightly depending on how "stiff" you want the mixture to be. If it's too dry, add more water. Polenta is extremely elastic. Mixing the polenta with a little water before adding it to the boiling water keeps it from becoming lumpy.

Stove-top cooking: Combine 1/2 cup cornmeal and 1/2 cup water in a bowl. Bring 2 cups of water to a boil in a medium saucepan. Stir in the polenta mixture. Reduce heat to the lowest setting, stirring continuously to prevent the polenta from sticking. Simmer on low for 10 minutes or until the polenta is thick and creamy. If it becomes too stiff or dry while cooking, add a small amount of water (1 to 2 tablespoons at a time) and keep stirring. Makes 2 cups.

Microwave cooking: In a 1-quart microwavable bowl, whisk together 1/2 cup polenta and 2 cups water. Cook in microwave on High for 3 minutes. Stir, and then microwave on High for an additional 2 minutes. Remove the polenta from the microwave, and let it rest for 1 minute. The polenta should be the consistency of pudding. If it appears watery, microwave for an additional 1 to 2 minutes. Makes 2 cups.

Rice   Whole grain brown rice is such a basic food that simply cooking it brings out its natural excellence for a satisfying meal. It takes about 40 to 45 minutes to prepare. That can be a problem when you're hungry and in a hurry. One solution is to create deliberate leftovers by cooking more rice than you need for one meal. Cooked rice will keep refrigerated for about 7 days, and you'll have a head start on future meals. One cup of raw brown rice yields 3 cups cooked.

Cook rice in a pot with a tight-fitting lid. Using a dented lid or one that is the wrong size lets too much water escape during cooking. Rinse 1 cup of rice and drain it, and then add 2 cups of fresh cool water to the pot. Cover and bring to a boil over the highest heat. When steam escapes from below the lid, turn off the heat for 5 minutes. Return to very low heat, and simmer for about 35 minutes or until the water has been absorbed. Remove from heat and let it sit, covered, for a few minutes before serving.

To cook white rice, use 1 3/4 cups water for each cup of rice and prepare as for brown rice. The water will be absorbed in

Grain Cooking Chart

1 cup Grain	Water (cups)	Cooking Time (minutes)	Yield (cups)
Barley	3	45	$3^1/_2$
Brown rice	2	45	3
Buckwheat	2	15	$2^1/_2$
Bulgur	2	15	$2^1/_2$
Couscous	1	10	$2^1/_3$
Kasha	2	15	$2^1/_2$
Millet	$2^3/_4$	40	$3^1/_2$
Quinoa	2	15	$2^1/_2$
White rice	$1^3/_4$	15	2
Wild rice	3	60	$2^2/_3$

15 to 20 minutes of cooking. One cup of white rice yields 2 cups cooked.

Use one of the following methods to reheat 1 cup of cooked rice.

On top of the stove: Heat rice in a covered saucepan on medium heat with 2 tablespoons of liquid for 4 to 5 minutes.

In the oven: Put rice in a baking dish. Add 2 tablespoons of liquid, and reheat in an oven set at 350 degrees F for 4 to 5 minutes.

In a microwave: Heat rice with 2 tablespoons of water. Cover the container; microwave on High 1 minute.

Steaming: Place the rice in a steamer basket over boiling water. Cover and steam for 2 minutes or until the rice is warm.

Cleaning the Pot

After removing cooked grains from the pot, you may notice a film that clings to the side of the saucepan. Fill the pot with water, and let it rest 30 minutes or overnight. When you wash the pot, the coating will practically slide off by itself.

Polenta with Mushroom Gravy

PREPARATION TIME: 15 minutes

This recipe is a two-part process, but it's straightforward and uncomplicated. Make a lick-your-plate meal in 15 minutes.

Polenta
1/2 cup cornmeal
1 1/2 cups water

Gravy
1 tablespoon olive oil
1 cup chopped onions
1/2 teaspoon dried thyme
2 cups sliced fresh mushrooms (about 4 large)
1 tablespoon flour
2/3 cup water, or white wine, or red wine
1 tablespoon soy sauce
Pepper

1. In a 1-quart microwave-safe bowl, whisk together the cornmeal and water. Cook in the microwave on High for 3 minutes. Whisk carefully (mixture will be hot); return the mixture to the microwave and cook 1 minute on High or until the polenta is thick and creamy. Remove from the microwave, and let the polenta rest while you cook the gravy.

2. Heat the oil in a small skillet on medium or medium-low heat. Sauté the onion and thyme for 6 minutes; stir occasionally. Add the mushrooms and continue to sauté on

medium heat until the mushrooms soften, stirring often, for 3 to 5 minutes. If the skillet becomes dry before the mushrooms are soft, add 1 tablespoon of water and continue cooking.

3. When the mushrooms are soft, add the flour and stir for a moment; then add the water and soy sauce. Simmer on medium-high, stirring until the sauce thickens, about 30 seconds to 1 minute. Remove from the heat.

4. Serve the polenta topped with gravy. Pepper to taste.

NOTE: This gravy is delicious ladled on mashed potatoes, rice, or noodles. If you choose to use water rather than wine, add 1 clove of finely chopped garlic when you add the mushrooms. Believe it or not, the water makes as tasty a gravy as the wine; they're just different.

Makes two servings

Polenta with Black Beans

PREPARATION TIME: 15 minutes

A mixture of cornmeal and water cooked as a mush is native to the Americas. The Italians adopted it as a staple of their cuisine and called it polenta. If you like pasta, you'll love polenta. It's the ultimate comfort food, and it's versatile, nourishing, and cheap. Cooked polenta can be topped with pasta sauce, sautéed or steamed vegetables, or cooked beans. It is often used as a stuffing and can be broiled or fried. It's lovely sprinkled with grated cheese. Polenta makes a delicious alternative to potatoes or rice. In this recipe, polenta is made on the stove, but if you have a microwave, it's even faster. (See Polenta with Mushroom Gravy on page 158.)

Beans
1 teaspoon olive oil
1/2 cup chopped onion (about 1/2 small)
2 cloves garlic, minced
1 teaspoon dried thyme
1 (14 1/2-ounce) can diced or ready-cut tomatoes, undrained
1 (15-ounce) can black beans, rinsed and drained

Polenta
1/2 cup cornmeal
2 cups water

Grated Parmesan cheese
1 tablespoon chopped fresh parsley (optional)

1. Heat the oil in a medium skillet over medium heat. Add the onion, garlic, and thyme. Sauté on medium heat for 3 to 5 minutes, until the onion is tender. Add the tomatoes and beans. Reduce the heat to low and gently simmer the bean mixture while you prepare the polenta.

2. In a small bowl, combine the cornmeal and 1/2 cup water. Set aside. In a medium saucepan, bring 11/2 cups water to a boil; pour in the cornmeal mixture and stir; reduce the heat to its lowest setting. Cook, stirring frequently, until the mixture is thick and smooth, about 10 minutes. If the polenta sticks to the bottom of the pot, add more water, 1 tablespoon at a time.

3. Serve beans and polenta side by side. Sprinkle with Parmesan cheese and chopped parsley if you desire.

Makes two to three servings

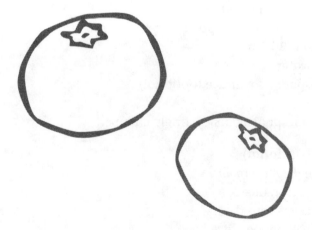

Kasha Pilaf

PREPARATION TIME: 10 minutes

COOKING TIME: 10 minutes

Kasha (or buckwheat groats) has a unique, earthy flavor, which you'll either like or you won't. There's not much middle ground between its fans and its detractors. Kasha can be a meal in itself, or it can be served as a side dish with steamed vegetables or baked tofu. It makes a tasty filling for baked squash and can take the place of rice or a potato on your plate. It's especially savory topped with gravy. The grain is ready to eat in 15 minutes.

1/4 cup kasha (buckwheat groats)
1 egg white, lightly beaten
1 tablespoon olive oil
1/4 cup onion, chopped
1 garlic clove, minced
1 cup mushrooms, chopped (two 3-inch mushrooms
     or four 2-inch)
1/2 cup water
1 1/2 teaspoons soy sauce (optional)
Pepper
1 to 2 tablespoons parsley, finely chopped

Extras (Optional)
Add with the mushrooms:
1/4 cup carrot, diced
1/4 cup celery, diced
1/4 cup bell pepper, diced

Add when the dish is finished cooking:
1/4 cup cooked bow-tie noodles or macaroni

1. In a small bowl, combine the egg white and kasha, and stir to coat the grain.

2. Heat oil on medium-high in small 8-inch skillet. Add the chopped onions and garlic, and sauté, stirring for 2 to 3 minutes until the onion is translucent. Add the mushrooms and one or two optional extras, if desired, and continue cooking, stirring until the mushrooms begin to give up their juice and look soft and shiny.

3. Add the kasha mixture to the skillet and stir well. Continue cooking for a minute or two on medium heat until the kasha kernels are separate and dry.

4. Mix the water and soy sauce together. Pour the mixture in the skillet. When the stock begins to simmer, cover and cook gently on low heat for about 10 to 15 minutes until the liquid is absorbed and the grain is soft. Adjust the seasoning; add pepper to taste and a splash of soy sauce if you desire. Garnish with fresh chopped parsley.

NOTE: The egg white creates a fluffier grain. Without it, the texture of the dish is more like porridge. You'll need a lid for the skillet in this recipe.

Makes one serving

Spontaneous Couscous

PREPARATION TIME: About 15 minutes

When liquid is added to this tiny mild-tasting grain, it magically puffs up and becomes tender in less than 10 minutes. Here couscous is energized with frozen green peas, tomatoes, and onions for a quick, light meal. If you desire, add Broiled Tofu (page 102) just before serving. Use about 2 cups of vegetables per serving and make substitutions at will. (Double the recipe, and chill leftovers for a ready-made salad for tomorrow, dressed with a vinaigrette dressing.)

1 teaspoon olive oil
1/2 medium onion, chopped (1 cup)
1/2 cup frozen peas
1/2 medium tomato, chopped
1/4 cup couscous
1/2 cup water
1 teaspoon finely chopped fresh parsley
Tabasco or fresh lemon juice (optional)

Salt and pepper

1. Heat the oil in a medium skillet. Sauté the onion on medium-low heat for 10 minutes or until the onions are lightly browned, stirring occasionally.

2. Add the peas, tomato, couscous, and water.

3. Cover and cook on low heat for 5 to 8 minutes, or until the peas are bright green, all the water is absorbed, and the couscous is soft. Add parsley.

4. Serve with a splash of Tabasco or fresh lemon juice, if desired. Salt and pepper to taste.

Makes one serving

Indian Rice

PREPARATION TIME: 12 minutes

Pineapple and banana make a perfect pair to flavor this sweet rice dish.

2 teaspoons vegetable oil
$1/2$ medium onion, chopped
$1/2$ medium carrot, thinly sliced on diagonal
$1/4$ green bell pepper, chopped
$1/4$ teaspoon curry powder
$1/4$ cup crushed pineapple
1 cup cooked rice
$1/2$ ripe banana, sliced
1 tablespoon raisins
Salt
1 tablespoon peanuts or cashews

1. Heat the oil in a large skillet over medium heat. Sauté the onion and carrot for 3 minutes. Add the bell pepper and curry, and sauté for another 2 minutes. Add the pineapple and rice; stir. Reduce the heat to low.
2. Gently stir in the banana and raisins, being careful not to mash the bananas. Cook until the bananas are warm, 1 or 2 minutes.
3. Salt to taste. Sprinkle with the peanuts. Serve.

Makes one serving

Beer and Aztec Rice

The ingredient list may look long, but the recipe is super simple, and the taste is fantastic.

1 tablespoon minced jalapeño chile
1/2 cup finely chopped onion
3 large cloves garlic, minced
1 1/2 teaspoons olive oil
1 tablespoon finely chopped fresh cilantro
1 1/2 teaspoons ground coriander
1/2 teaspoon ground cumin
1 cup brown rice
1 cup water
1 cup dark beer, ale, or stout
1/4 teaspoon salt
1/2 cup frozen peas, thawed

1. If you like food really hot, leave a few of the seeds in the jalapeño. If you like a mild flavor, remove the seeds and vein. In a medium saucepan, sauté the jalapeño, onion, and garlic in olive oil until the onion softens, about 5 minutes. Add the cilantro, coriander, and cumin and sauté about 1 minute.

2. Add the rice, water, beer, and salt. Bring the pot to a boil. Reduce the heat and cover. Cook on low heat for 35 to 40 minutes, until the rice is tender. When the rice is nearly done and the liquid is almost gone, turn off the heat and let the rice sit on the burner for another 5 minutes.

3. Remove the pot from heat and stir in the peas. Re-cover the pot and let it sit for 5 minutes to warm the peas. Serve.

Makes three servings

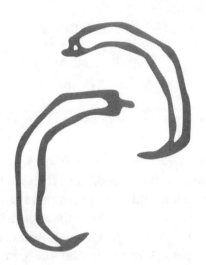

Chinese Fried Rice

PREPARATION TIME: 10 minutes

MARINATING TIME: About 10 minutes

This recipe happily accepts substitutions. Use whatever vegetables you have on hand—broccoli, snow peas, or carrots are good choices.

2 tablespoons soy sauce
2 teaspoons sugar
1/4 block extra-firm tofu
1 teaspoon vegetable oil
1/4 medium green bell pepper, cut into thin strips (about 1/4 cup)
1 cup cooked rice
1/4 cup frozen peas
1 scallion, thinly sliced (about 1/4 cup)

1. In a shallow bowl, mix together the soy sauce and sugar. Cut the tofu into strips about 1/2 inch wide. Marinate for about 10 minutes in the soy and sugar mixture.

2. After the tofu has marinated, heat the oil in a large skillet over medium heat. Add the bell pepper, stir, and fry for 1 to 2 minutes. Remove the tofu from the marinade and add the tofu to the skillet. Stir for a moment. Add the rice and heat thoroughly, about 1 minute. Add the peas and scallion, and stir.

3. Taste. If you desire, top the dish with some of the remaining marinade. Serve immediately.

NOTE: If you have time, press the tofu to remove excess water for 15 minutes before you marinate it. See directions on page 16.

Makes one serving

Rice with Garbanzo Beans

PREPARATION TIME: 10 minutes

Traditional Mediterranean flavors give a cup of rice great taste.

1 teaspoon olive oil
1/2 cup finely chopped onion
1 clove garlic, finely chopped
1 cup tightly packed, washed, chopped spinach
1 tablespoon fresh lemon juice
1/4 cup garbanzo beans
1/2 medium tomato, chopped (about 1/2 cup)
1/2 teaspoon dried thyme
1 cup cooked rice
2 to 4 tablespoons crumbled feta cheese
Salt and pepper

1. Heat the oil in a medium skillet over medium heat. Add the onion and garlic and sauté for about 3 minutes, until the onion softens.

2. Stir in the spinach, lemon juice, garbanzo beans, tomato, and thyme. Add rice, cover, and cook for 2 to 3 minutes, stirring occasionally.

3. When the spinach has wilted and the rice is hot, serve topped with crumbled feta cheese. Salt and pepper to taste.

Makes one serving

Rice Vera Cruz

PREPARATION TIME: 6 minutes

COOKING TIME: About 8 minutes

This dish can be the center of your meal or complement a bowl of chili.

2 teaspoons vegetable oil
1/4 cup frozen corn
1 teaspoon seeded and minced jalapeño chile
1/2 teaspoon ground cumin
1/2 medium tomato, diced
2 scallions, finely chopped
1 tablespoon finely chopped fresh cilantro
2 cups cooked rice
Salt

1. In a medium skillet on medium heat, warm the oil. Add the corn, jalapeño, and cumin; cover and cook on low heat for 3 to 5 minutes, stirring occasionally.

2. Stir in the tomato, scallions, cilantro, and rice. Cook on low heat for 3 to 5 minutes until hot. Stir occasionally. Add a dash or two of water if needed to prevent the rice from sticking.

3. Salt to taste and serve.

Makes two servings

CHAPTER 10

Noodles

When you are busy and overworked, noodles can become one of your best friends; there are dozens of different kinds and shapes from which to choose (and don't forget full-bodied whole wheat varieties or delicate rice noodles). Ready-made pasta sauce straight from a jar is tasty, but it becomes boring as a steady diet. The following recipes will make you a versatile pasta cook, and you can prepare great toppings in the same amount of time it takes to cook the noodles. Add a fresh green salad with your pasta, and you'll have a whole meal.

Super-Excellent Pasta

To make one serving of pasta, use about 4 ounces of noodles. Bring 3 quarts of water to a rapid boil. Make sure you have enough water in the pot to allow the pasta to swim freely while it cooks. Add the pasta to the boiling water. Stir once with a long-handled wooden spoon to keep the pieces from sticking together; cover the pot so that the water will quickly return to a boil. (If you taste-test pasta dangling from a wooden spoon, you won't burn your lips or tongue on a hot metal utensil.) When the water boils, remove the lid and stir once again. The directions on packages of pasta usually over-cook the noodles, so begin checking for doneness after about 5 minutes of cooking. For pasta served hot, cook it al dente, or just to the point where there is a slight resistance or "tooth" when you bite it. Drain cooked pasta immediately. Don't run cold water over it, because the outer layer of starch that remains helps the sauce stick. When you make pasta for cold salads, do rinse the cooked noodles.

Rice Noodles

You will find rice noodles in Asian markets and well-stocked supermarkets. They are great in clear soups, topped with your favorite pasta sauce, added to stir-fries, or in Thailand's best-known noodle dish—pad Thai. They're ready to eat in about 8 minutes.

To cook, place the noodles in boiling water and boil for 5 minutes; add salt and continue boiling for an additional 2 to 3 minutes or until translucent. Drain and rinse in cold water.

Whole Wheat Pasta
with Arugula

PREPARATION TIME: 10 minutes

Arugula is a green with lots of pizzazz! It's a gourmet standard for salads, and here its sharp, peppery taste adds snap to pasta. Make a lot. It's great reheated in your microwave for lunch the next day or eaten cold from the container. The more often you make this recipe, the more arugula you'll find you want to toss into the bowl.

2 to 2¹/₂ tablespoons olive oil
1 to 2 large cloves garlic, minced
¹/₄ pound uncooked whole wheat pasta (any shapes)
1 to 2 cups arugula (use more if you like)
¹/₄ cup black olives, pitted and sliced thin
1 large tomato, chopped in bite-size pieces
Salt and pepper
¹/₄ cup Parmesan cheese (optional)

1. Mix oil and garlic in a large bowl.

2. Wash arugula, spin or pat dry, cut off the larger stems, and discard; slice or chop the leaves into bite-size pieces.

3. Cook pasta al dente; begin checking for doneness after 5 minutes. Drain (don't rinse!), and add immediately to oil and garlic. Toss.

4. Add olives, tomato, and arugula. Salt and pepper to taste, and sprinkle with Parmesan, if desired. Lightly toss; serve immediately.

Makes one serving

Pasta with Green Beans and Feta Cheese

PREPARATION TIME: 12 minutes

The classic flavors of green beans and feta cheese combine in this dish to make a truly simple yet outstanding meal. Buy a bag of frozen green beans. It's easier to scoop out what you need from a bag than a cardboard box.

1/4 pound uncooked pasta
1 teaspoon olive oil
1/4 cup thinly sliced onion
1 large or 2 small cloves garlic, minced
1/8 teaspoon dried basil
1 1/2 cups frozen French-cut green beans
1 medium chopped tomato (about 1 cup)
1 tablespoon crumbled feta cheese
Salt and pepper

1. Bring a covered pot of water to a rapid boil, stir in the pasta, and cover until the water returns to a boil. Uncover the pot and cook the pasta until al dente, 8 to 10 minutes.

2. While the pasta cooks, heat the oil in a medium skillet over medium heat. Add the onion, garlic, and basil; sauté until the onion is soft, 3 to 4 minutes, stirring occasionally. Add the green beans and stir. Cover and cook on medium-low heat until the beans are hot and crisp-tender, about 5 minutes. Just before you serve the beans, stir in the fresh tomato.

3. When the pasta is al dente, drain and serve topped with the green bean sauce. Sprinkle generously with feta cheese and season with salt and pepper to taste.

Makes one serving

Pasta with Zucchini and Basil

Preparation Time: 12 minutes

Zucchini is a vegetable that has an affinity for pasta.

1/4 pound uncooked spaghetti
1 teaspoon olive oil
2 to 3 cloves garlic, finely chopped
1 small or 1/2 medium zucchini, sliced (about 1 cup)
1/4 teaspoon dried basil
Salt and pepper
2 teaspoons fresh lemon juice
Grated Parmesan cheese

1. Bring a covered pot of water to a rapid boil. Stir in the pasta, and cover the pot until the water returns to a boil. Uncover and cook until the pasta is al dente (begin checking for doneness after about 5 minutes of cooking).

2. While the pasta cooks, heat the oil in a medium skillet over medium-high heat. Add the garlic, zucchini, and basil. Quickly fry until the zucchini begins to brown, about 5 minutes, stirring occasionally. Add the lemon juice and stir. Remove from the heat.

3. When the pasta is al dente, drain it. Place the hot pasta on a warm plate; top with zucchini and grated Parmesan cheese. Lightly toss. Salt and pepper to taste.

Makes one serving

Farfalle and Peas

PREPARATION TIME: 20 minutes

Farfalle is the Italian name for bow-tie pasta. The nooks and crannies in the bow ties help hold the peas on your fork. The 15-minute onion sauté gives this simple dish great flavor.

2 teaspoons olive oil
1 small onion, chopped (about 1 cup)
1 cup frozen peas
Salt and pepper
2 cups uncooked bow-tie pasta
Grated Parmesan cheese (optional)

1. Bring a covered pot of water to a rapid boil. While the water comes to a boil, heat the oil in a medium skillet over medium heat. Add the onion, and lower the heat to medium-low; sauté for 10 to 15 minutes, stirring occasionally. (This long, slow sauté is what gives this dish its great flavor.) When the onion begins to turn brown, add the peas and salt and pepper to taste. Stir. Cook for 1 or 2 minutes. Cover and turn off the heat, leaving the skillet on the burner while the pasta finishes cooking.

2. When the pot of water boils, stir in the pasta, and re-cover the pot for a moment until the water returns to a boil. Uncover the pot. As soon as the pasta is cooked al dente (begin checking for doneness after about 5 minutes), drain it. Bow-tie pasta may take a few minutes longer to cook than spaghetti.

3. Serve the pasta topped with the onion and peas. Sprinkle with Parmesan cheese, if you desire.

Makes one serving

Pasta Primavera

PREPARATION TIME: 10 minutes

Here is a pasta vegetable medley for two. Don't let the ingredient list scare you. It takes only 5 minutes to chop the vegetables.

1/2 pound uncooked spaghetti
1 tablespoon olive oil
1/2 medium onion, chopped (about 1/2 cup)
1 clove garlic, minced
1/2 medium carrot, thinly sliced
1/4 green bell pepper, chopped
4 mushrooms, sliced (about 1 cup)
1 medium zucchini, sliced (about 1 cup)
1/4 teaspoon dried basil
1/8 teaspoon dried oregano
1/2 medium tomato, chopped
2 tablespoons water
2 to 4 teaspoons fresh lemon juice (optional)
Grated Parmesan cheese
Salt and pepper

1. Bring a covered pot of water to a rapid boil, stir in the pasta, and cover until the water returns to a boil. Uncover the pot and cook the pasta until al dente; begin checking for doneness after 5 minutes.

2. While the pasta cooks, heat the oil in a medium skillet over medium heat. Add the onion, garlic, and carrot; sauté until the onion is soft, about 3 minutes. Add the bell pepper, mushrooms, zucchini, basil, and oregano; sauté, stirring occasionally until the vegetables begin to soften, about 3 min-

utes. Add the tomato and 2 tablespoons of water; cover and cook for 3 minutes or until the vegetables are just tender. Uncover, stir, and remove from the heat.

3. When the pasta is al dente, drain it. Serve the pasta topped with the vegetable mixture. Sprinkle each serving with a splash of fresh lemon juice, if desired, and grated Parmesan cheese. Salt and pepper to taste.

Makes two servings

Pasta with
Garbanzo Beans

PREPARATION TIME: 15 minutes

The buttery flavor of garbanzo beans makes rich-tasting pasta.
If you're out of spinach, use a chopped fresh tomato instead.
Either way, it's delicious.

1/4 pound uncooked spaghetti
2 teaspoons olive oil
1/2 medium onion, chopped (about 1/2 cup)
1 large clove garlic, minced
1/2 teaspoon dried dill
2 cups tightly packed, chopped spinach
1/4 cup canned garbanzo beans, rinsed and drained
2 tablespoon fresh lemon juice
Grated Parmesan cheese
Salt and pepper

1. Bring a covered pot of water to a rapid boil. When the
   water comes to a rolling boil, stir in the pasta; re-cover the
   pot, and return it to a boil. Uncover the pot and cook the
   pasta al dente (begin checking for doneness after about 5
   minutes of cooking).

2. Heat the oil in a medium skillet on medium heat. Sauté the onion, garlic, and dill for about 5 minutes, stirring occasionally until the onion softens. Add the spinach and garbanzo beans and continue cooking, stirring until the spinach wilts, about 3 minutes.

3. When the pasta is al dente, drain it. Serve the pasta topped with the spinach mixture. Sprinkle with lemon juice and grated Parmesan cheese. Salt and pepper to taste.

Makes one serving

Pasta with Greens

PREPARATION TIME: 10 minutes

Whip up this fabulous meal and enjoy the rich taste of tender greens and creamy cottage cheese tossed with pasta.

1/4 pound uncooked spaghetti
1 cup tightly packed kale or spinach
2 teaspoons vegetable oil
1 tablespoon water
1/2 cup nonfat cottage cheese
2 cloves garlic, minced
1 tablespoon chopped walnuts
Salt and pepper

1. Bring a large covered pot of water to a rapid boil. Add the pasta, stir, and cover the pot until the water returns to a boil. Uncover the pot and continue cooking until the pasta is al dente (begin checking for doneness after about 5 minutes of cooking).

2. Wash the kale and remove the tough center stems. Chop the leaves into bite-size pieces. Heat the oil in a medium skillet on medium-high heat; add the kale and sauté, stirring for 2 minutes. Add 1 tablespoon of water, cover, and cook until kale is wilted and still bright green, 3 to 5 minutes. Turn off the heat and stir in the cottage cheese and garlic.

3. When the pasta is al dente, drain it, and serve it tossed with the kale mixture. Sprinkle with walnuts. Salt and pepper to taste.

Makes one serving

Classic Tomato Sauce

PREPARATION TIME: 15 minutes

COOKING TIME: 15 minutes

Use this sauce for pasta, lasagna, or your favorite pizza. Commercial sauce is convenient when you're short on time, but it won't match the flavor of one you make yourself.

1/2 medium onion, finely chopped (about 1 cup)
3 cloves garlic, minced
2 teaspoons olive oil
1 (28-ounce) can whole tomatoes with juice (about 3 cups)
Salt and pepper

Extras (Optional)
2 teaspoons dried basil (3 tablespoons chopped fresh)
1/4 teaspoon dried oregano
1 tablespoon chopped fresh parsley

1. In a medium skillet, sauté onions and garlic in oil on medium heat until the onions are translucent, about 10 minutes.
2. Drain the tomato juice into the pan with the onions. Use your hands and gently squeeze the tomatoes into the skillet. Add one or more of the optional extras, if desired.
3. Simmer for 15 minutes uncovered, stirring occasionally. Salt and pepper to taste.

Makes 3 cups

Peanut Pasta

Preparation Time: 12 minutes

Boil up a pot of pasta and choose a sauce. Either one of these sauces can be ready in minutes without any cooking. Peanut sauce is also good served over cooked rice, baked sweet potatoes, and a variety of steamed vegetables.

1/4 pound uncooked spaghetti or linguini
1 cup broccoli florets
1/2 medium carrot, thinly sliced (about 1/2 cup)
1 cup thinly sliced Chinese cabbage
1 scallion finely chopped (about 1 tablespoon)

Peanut Sauce with Tahini
1 tablespoon peanut butter
1 tablespoon tahini
1 tablespoon apple cider vinegar
1 to 2 tablespoons orange juice
1 teaspoon soy sauce

Peanut Sauce with Salsa
2 tablespoons peanut butter
2 tablespoons fresh lemon juice
2 tablespoons prepared Mexican red salsa
1 teaspoon brown sugar
Salt

1. Bring a covered pot of water to a rapid boil. While the water is heating, choose one of the sauces, and mix together the sauce ingredients in a small bowl until smooth and creamy. Add more juice if necessary.

2. When the water boils, stir in the pasta, cover the pot, and return it to a boil. Uncover the pot and cook until the noodles are al dente or just tender (begin checking for doneness after about 5 minutes of cooking).

3. While the noodles cook, steam the vegetables in a steamer basket placed in a pot or in a steamer. Add water to the pot and bring it to a boil, then add the broccoli and carrot; steam for 1¹/₂ to 2 minutes. Add the cabbage; steam for another 30 seconds or until the vegetables are crisp-tender. Make sure the water does not touch the vegetables while they cook.

4. When pasta is al dente, drain it, and serve it immediately tossed with the vegetables and sauce. Garnish with chopped scallion.

Makes one serving

Pad Thai

PREPARATION TIME: 20 minutes

Making pad Thai is easier than you might imagine. It's essentially a stir-fry with rice noodles. This recipe calls for mung bean sprouts. They are the sprouts you find in nearly every supermarket. The chile in this recipe is the ordinary little jalapeño chile. If you like your food hot, leave in some of the seeds, but look out! The hardest part of this recipe is hand-grating two carrots.

Noodles
2 quarts water
6 ounces rice noodles ($1/4$ inch wide)

Sauce
3 tablespoons fresh lemon or lime juice
3 tablespoons catsup
1 tablespoon sugar
$1/2$ cup soy sauce

Stir-Fry
1 to 2 tablespoons vegetable oil
4 large cloves garlic, minced
1 medium fresh green jalapeño chile, seeded and minced
2 medium carrots, grated (about 2 cups)
$1/2$ pound mung bean sprouts (about $1 1/2$ cups)
4 scallions, finely chopped (about $3/4$ cup)
2 tablespoons chopped peanuts
2 tablespoons finely chopped fresh cilantro or parsley
    (optional)

1. In a covered pan, bring the water to a rolling boil; stir in the rice noodles, and cook for 5 to 7 minutes. Drain the noodles, rinse them well under cool water, and set aside.

2. In a small bowl, combine the sauce ingredients; set aside.

3. Heat the oil in a medium skillet on medium-high heat. Add the garlic and jalapeño; stir and fry for a moment. Stir in the grated carrots. Stir and fry for 1 to 2 minutes. Add the sauce, noodles, bean sprouts, and scallions. Stir everything together. When the ingredients are warm, about 1 minute, remove to a platter. Garnish with the peanuts and cilantro, if you desire.

NOTE: Just before you're ready to add the noodles to the carrot mixture, check to see whether they're sticking together. If they are, quickly rinse and drain them again. They'll immediately come apart.

Makes two or three servings

CHAPTER 11

Various Vegetables
and Stir-Fries

According to the book *Potatoes,* by Alvin and Virginia B. Silverstein, Frederick the Great of Prussia decreed in 1744 that anyone who refused to grow and eat potatoes would have their ears and nose cut off. You may not have time to grow potatoes, but you'll find delicious vegetable meals in this chapter, along with the how-to's of artichoke eating.

Deconstructed Artichoke

PREPARATION TIME: 5 minutes

COOKING TIME: 30 to 40 minutes

If you are looking for an entertaining meal and you like eating with your fingers, this strange-looking vegetable is for you. Cook the artichoke, and then just do what comes naturally. Pull off a leaf and dunk it in sauce. Put the leaf in your mouth and pull it through your teeth, scraping off the tender flesh. Discard what's left, and pull off another leaf. When you get to the center, scoop out and discard the thistle-like "choke." What's left under the choke is the soft "heart." It's the best part. Cut the heart into bite-size pieces and dunk it into the sauce. Tsiziki Sauce (page 43) and Tahini Sauce (page 44) are both excellent choices.

1 globe artichoke
2 tablespoons fresh lemon juice or wine vinegar
1 teaspoon olive oil
1 clove garlic

1. Cut off the stem of the artichoke so it will sit evenly on the bottom of a pot. Stand the artichoke up in the pot with 3 inches of water. Add the lemon juice or vinegar, oil, and garlic; cover the pot and bring it to a boil. Reduce the heat and simmer until the stem end is tender or a leaf can be removed with the slightest resistance (about 40 minutes). Check the pot from time to time to see whether the water has boiled away. Add more water if necessary.

2. When the artichoke is done, drain it well, and serve it hot, warm, or at room temperature. Most people enjoy dipping the leaves in sauce or melted butter, but it's tasty unadorned, too.

Makes one serving

Easy Asparagus

PREPARATION TIME: 5 minutes

COOKING TIME: About 20 minutes

Asparagus is a divine vegetable that arrives in the produce department in the spring. Eat it as a salad or as a side dish with a sandwich.

1/2 pound fresh asparagus
1 teaspoon olive oil
Salt
Lemon juice

Preheat the oven to 400 degrees F.

1. Wash the asparagus and snap off the tough ends of the stalks. Hold the stalk with the thumb and index finger of both hands, and the woody part will break off naturally in the right spot.

2. Place the asparagus on a baking sheet and drizzle the olive oil over the spears. Sprinkle with salt and roll the asparagus around until it is lightly coated with the oil.

3. Bake for about 10 minutes. When the stalks are slightly blistered, turn them over. Total roasting time will vary depending on the thickness of the stalks. Cook until tender, 10 to 15 minutes. Serve sprinkled with a few drops of lemon juice, or dip the spears in Tsiziki Sauce (page 43) if you desire.

NOTE: You can also cook asparagus by steaming it over boiling water for 3 to 6 minutes or by simmering it in water until it is tender.

Makes one or two servings

Steamed Vegetable Combo

PREPARATION TIME: **8 minutes**

Enjoy steamed vegetables as a stand-alone one-bowl meal, or pair them with a variety of other dishes. The trick to making them taste good is to avoid overcooking. Begin checking for doneness in 2 minutes. The vegetables should be crisp-tender when done. Chilled and dressed with a vinaigrette dressing, a splash of balsamic vinegar, or a squeeze of lemon juice and seasoned to taste with salt and pepper, steamed vegetables make a salad, or serve them hot, topped with creamy Tsiziki Sauce (page 43) or Tahini Sauce (page 44) if you wish.

1/2 cup sliced carrots, cut 1/2-inch thick (1 carrot)
1/2 cup broccoli florets (1-inch pieces)
1/2 cup cauliflower florets (1-inch pieces)
Salt and pepper

1. Arrange the vegetables in a steamer over boiling water.

2. Cover and steam 4 to 5 minutes or until crisp-tender. Salt and pepper to taste.

Makes one serving

Roasted Red Bell Pepper

PREPARATION TIME: 3 minutes

COOKING TIME: 8 to 15 minutes

Red bell peppers take on a whole new personality when roasted or slowly sautéed. Each cooking method produces a special taste; both are delicious. Once you've discovered their sweet flavor, they'll become a mainstay in your vegetarian eating. They are cheapest in the fall. Use them on sandwiches, crackers, cooked pasta, green salads, baked potatoes, in stir-fries, and with cooked grains. Anywhere they land, they're luscious.

1 red bell pepper
2 teaspoons olive oil

Preheat the broiler.

To Roast
1. Cut the pepper in half lengthwise. Discard the seeds and membranes. Place the pepper on a baking sheet with its shiny skin side facing up. Broil 3 or 4 inches from the heat for 8 to 10 minutes or until the skin is blackened and charred.

2. Remove the pepper from the oven. Seal it in a paper bag to steam for 10 minutes. (It works even if you skip the paper bag trick.) Peel and discard the charred skin. Do not rinse; that will wash away the smoky taste. Slice roasted peppers into lengthwise strips. Drizzle with a little oil.

To Sauté

1. Cut the pepper in half lengthwise. Discard the seeds and membranes. Slice the pepper into lengthwise strips.

2. Heat oil in a small skillet on medium heat. Sauté the pepper on medium or medium-low heat for 15 minutes, stirring frequently until tender and lightly browned.

NOTE: Cooked peppers will keep for a week stored covered in the refrigerator.

Makes about 1/2 cup

Acorn Squash Bake
(or Microwave)

PREPARATION TIME: 8 minutes

COOKING TIME: 40 to 45 minutes (or Microwave: 8 to 10 minutes)

Acorn squash is one of the tastiest in the fall harvest. Serve it as a side dish with baked tofu or refried beans. If you like squash extra-sweet, spoon on Orange Raisin Sauce (see recipe below).

1 acorn squash, split lengthwise and seeded
1 teaspoon olive oil

Orange Raisin Sauce
1/4 cup raisins
1/4 cup orange juice
1 tablespoon brown sugar
1/4 teaspoon cinnamon

Preheat oven to 350 degress F.

1. Place squash cut side down in an oiled baking dish. Bake 40 to 45 minutes or until tender.

2. In a small pan on medium-high heat, combine raisins, orange juice, sugar, and cinnamon. Warm the mixture until it just begins to simmer. Remove from heat and let it sit for 5 minutes. Spoon over the top of the cooked squash.

NOTE: To microwave instead of baking, place squash cut side down in a microwave-safe dish. Add 1/4 cup of water. Microwave on High 8 to 10 minutes or until tender

Makes two servings

Sweet Potato Fries

PREPARATION TIME: 2 minutes

COOKING TIME: 10 to 15 minutes

The irresistible, rich flavor of sweet potatoes (often called yams) makes them great for broiling.

1 sweet potato or yam
1 to 2 tablespoons vegetable oil
Salt

1. Preheat oven to broiler setting. Cut the potato in half and then into French-fry shaped strips along the length of the potato. (No need to peel the potato, but wash the skin before you slice it.)

2. Place the fries in a large bowl. Add the olive oil, and stir to evenly coat the potatoes.

3. Spread the fries onto a baking sheet; avoid building a thick layer. If piled high, the potatoes will steam, not broil. Place the potatoes in the broiler section of the oven on a shelf 3 to 4 inches from the top. Broil the potatoes 8 to 10 minutes, turning them once or twice until they are lightly browned.

4. Reset the oven to 400 degrees. Transfer the fries from the broiler portion of the oven to the center of the oven. Bake for 10 to 15 minutes. Sprinkle with salt and serve.

NOTE: Use this recipe to make "fries" from russet potatoes, white potatoes, and red potatoes.

Makes two servings

Gingered Chinese Greens Stir-Fry

PREPARATION TIME: 15 minutes

TOFU PRESSING TIME: 15 to 20 minutes

Serve this simple, crisp stir-fry over warm rice or cooked noodles. (The chili oil in this recipe may also be labeled red oil, hot oil, or hot pepper oil.)

1/2 cake Chinese-style firm tofu (about 7 ounces)
2 cups packed shredded Chinese cabbage or bok choy
     (4 or 5 leaves)
2 teaspoons vegetable oil
1/2 teaspoon minced or grated gingerroot
1 to 2 teaspoons water
Splash of chili oil
1 tablespoon finely chopped fresh cilantro

Sauce
1 tablespoon soy sauce
3 tablespoons orange juice
1 tablespoon fresh lemon or lime juice
1 tablespoon water
1 teaspoon sugar
1/2 teaspoon cornstarch

1. Sandwich the tofu between two plates. Top with a heavy book. Let sit for 15 to 20 minutes. Remove the weight and top cover, and drain the water from the bottom plate. The tofu is now ready to use. Cut the tofu into 1/2-inch cubes.

2. Wash and thinly slice the cabbage leaves and stems. Heat oil in a medium skillet over medium-high heat. Add ginger and cabbage. Stir and fry for about 2 minutes. Add water; cover and cook over medium heat until cabbage is soft, about 2 to 3 minutes.

3. In a small bowl, combine the sauce ingredients. Add the tofu and sauce to the skillet and gently stir until the sauce thickens, about 2 minutes. Serve immediately; splash with hot chili oil and cilantro.

NOTE: If you don't have chili oil, make this recipe anyway. (Substitute Tabasco for chili oil if you desire.)

Makes one serving

Tofu Cabbage Stir-Fry

PREPARATION TIME: 15 to 20 minutes

Here is a fast meal for breakfast, lunch, or dinner on a cold winter day. The pressed tofu becomes golden brown and crispy in this stir-fry. If you don't have sesame seeds, go for it anyway.

1/3 block (4 to 5 ounces) firm tofu
2 teaspoons toasted sesame oil or vegetable oil
1 large clove garlic, minced
1 teaspoon minced fresh ginger
2 cups shredded green or red cabbage (about 1/4 small head)
Salt and pepper or soy sauce
1 teaspoon sesame seeds, toasted

1. Sandwich the tofu between two plates. Top with a heavy book. Let sit for 15 to 20 minutes. Remove the weight and top cover, and drain the water from the bottom plate. The tofu is now ready to use. Cut the tofu into 1/2-inch cubes.

2. Heat 1 teaspoon of the oil in a medium skillet over medium-high heat. Add the tofu and stir and fry until lightly browned, 3 to 4 minutes. Add the garlic and ginger; sauté 1 minute longer. Remove the tofu from the skillet and set aside.

3. Re-oil the skillet with the remaining oil, and cook the cabbage over medium-high heat until soft, 3 to 5 minutes. Add the tofu. Remove the skillet from the heat. Season with salt and pepper or a splash of soy sauce. Serve when everything is hot. Sprinkle with toasted sesame seeds.

NOTE: To toast sesame seeds, place the seeds in a dry skillet on medium-high heat for 1 to 2 minutes. Watch the seeds carefully; they toast quickly. Stir the seeds and shake the pan frequently; when the seeds are golden, immediately remove them from the skillet.

Makes one serving

Assorted Vegetable
Stir-Fry

PREPARATION TIME: 15 minutes

Have you ever wondered how Chinese restaurants get their stir-fries to glisten? The secret is in a sauce made with cornstarch. Choose one of the following sauce recipes, and serve the stir-fry over a bed of cooked rice, pasta, or noodles.

Sweet and Sour Sauce
1 tablespoon soy sauce
1 tablespoon white vinegar
1 tablespoon catsup
2 teaspoons sugar
1/4 cup water
1 teaspoon cornstarch

Tangy Sauce
1 tablespoon hoisin sauce
1 tablespoon white vinegar
1 tablespoon soy sauce
1/4 cup water
1 teaspoon cornstarch

Stir-Fry
2 teaspoons vegetable oil
1 clove garlic, minced
1 medium carrot diagonally sliced (about 1 cup)
1/2 bell pepper, seeded and chopped, or 12 snow peas
1/2 medium zucchini, diagonally sliced (about 1 cup)
1 tablespoon finely chopped scallion (optional)

1. Choose one of the sauces, and combine the sauce ingredients in a small bowl.

2. Heat the oil in a medium skillet over medium-high heat. Add the garlic and swirl it in the oil for a moment. Add the carrot, bell pepper, and zucchini; stir and fry for 3 to 4 minutes.

3. Stir the sauce and pour it over the vegetables; stir and simmer for about 30 seconds or until the sauce thickens and the vegetables become glazed. Serve immediately. Garnish with chopped scallion if you desire.

Makes one serving

Broccoli, Carrot, and Cashew Stir-Fry

PREPARATION TIME: 10 minutes

Almost any combination of vegetables works in a stir-fry. Figure on 2 to 2¹/₂ cups of cut, raw vegetables per serving. If that seems like a lot, remember that vegetables shrink from water loss during cooking. If you can't find extra-firm tofu, firm will work.

3 ounces extra-firm tofu
2 teaspoons vegetable oil
1 clove garlic, finely chopped
1 carrot, diagonally sliced (1 cup)
1¹/₂ cups broccoli florets
1 tablespoon soy sauce
2 tablespoons chopped scallion (1 small)
2 tablespoons coarsely chopped cashews

1. Blot the tofu between paper towels, and then cut it into ¹/₂-inch cubes.

2. Heat the oil in a medium skillet on medium-high heat. Add the garlic and swirl it in the oil for 30 seconds; add the tofu, carrot, and broccoli. Stir and fry for about 3 minutes. Add the soy sauce; stir and fry for about 30 seconds.

3. Serve immediately. Garnish with the scallion and cashews.

Makes one serving

Roasted Vegetable Rush

PREPARATION TIME: 12 minutes

COOKING TIME: 15 minutes

These brown and crispy potatoes take center stage, and the vegetables are sweet and caramelized.

3 medium red potatoes (cut into 1-inch cubes)
3 mushrooms, quartered (about 1 cup)
3/4 green bell pepper, cut into bite-size chunks
5 cloves garlic, coarsely chopped
1 tablespoon olive oil
1 teaspoon dried rosemary
1 tablespoon fresh lemon juice or balsamic vinegar
Salt and pepper

Preheat the broiler.

1. Cook the potato cubes in a pot of rapidly boiling water for 5 minutes. Drain thoroughly. Place the mushrooms, bell pepper, garlic, and cooked potatoes in a large bowl. Add the olive oil and rosemary, and stir to evenly coat the vegetables with oil.

2. Spread the vegetables onto a baking sheet, but avoid building a thick layer; if piled high, the vegetables will steam not broil.

3. Broil vegetables for 10 minutes, until well cooked but not burned. Stir once or twice to ensure even cooking. Serve the vegetables with a splash of fresh lemon juice or balsamic vinegar. Salt and pepper to taste.

Makes one or two servings

Potato Skillet Hash

PREPARATION TIME: 10 minutes

COOKING TIME: 20 minutes

This meal turns heads in restaurants. If you didn't order it, it's the one you'll wish you had. Make the dish at home for breakfast, lunch, or dinner. Add more heat with a splash of Tabasco if you desire.

1 tablespoon olive oil
1 medium potato, diced (cut into 1/2-inch cubes)
   (about 2 cups)
1/3 cup carrot, thinly sliced
1/3 cup medium green bell pepper, chopped
3/4 cup onion, chopped
2 tablespoons water
1/2 teaspoon dried thyme
Salt and pepper

1. Heat the oil in a heavy skillet over medium-high heat. Add the potatoes, carrot, bell pepper, and onion; sauté for 5 to 7 minutes, stirring frequently.

2. Add the water. Reduce the heat to medium-low; cover and cook for 10 minutes or until the potatoes are tender.

3. Remove the lid. Add the thyme and stir. Continue cooking for 1 minute. If there is water in the pan, cook 1 minute longer or until the water evaporates. Remove from heat; salt and pepper to taste.

Makes one to two servings

Basic Baked Potatoes

PREPARATION TIME: 1 minute

COOKING TIME: 45 to 60 minutes

Turn a baked potato into a banquet. Top it with sautéed or roasted vegetables, chili, spaghetti sauce, a ladle of soup, or a dollop of non-fat plain yogurt. Just don't do it all at the same time.

1 or more russet potatoes
Vegetable oil (optional)

Preheat the oven to 400 degrees F.

Wash the potatoes, dry them, and rub with oil if you desire. Pierce the skin with a knife before baking to allow the steam that forms inside as they cook to escape. Otherwise, they may explode. Bake for about 60 minutes until fork-piercing tender. (If you want to speed up the process, cut the potato in half lengthwise and bake cut side down on a baking sheet for 45 minutes until soft.)

NOTE: Bake two potatoes at the same time and store the extra in the refrigerator. When you're in a hurry, you'll have one ready to go. Reheat it in a microwave for a quick meal or snack, or moisten the potato and reheat it in an oven at 350 degrees F for 15 minutes.

Makes one serving

Five-Minute Microwave-Baked Potato

PREPARATION TIME: 1 minute

COOKING TIME: 5 minutes

If you are in a hurry and have a microwave, you can bake a potato in about 5 minutes.

1 potato

1. Wash and dry the potato and pierce the skin in several places.
2. Microwave on High for 5 minutes. Remove the potato from the microwave, and let rest, covered, for 5 minutes. Squeeze the skin to see if the potato is soft. If it is, it's ready to eat. If it feels hard, return it to the microwave and heat on High for another minute. (It's better to undercook the potato, test for doneness, and return it to the microwave if necessary, than to overcook it. Overcooked microwaved potatoes shrivel and become pasty.) Because of the size of the potato and the power of the microwave, cooking times may vary.

NOTE: You can also microwave a sweet potato or yam. Pierce the skin several times and cook on High for 4 to 6 minutes. Let it sit for 3 to 4 minutes before serving.

Makes one serving

Mashed Potatoes

PREPARATION TIME: 6 minutes

COOKING TIME: About 15 minutes

*Here is a real comfort food. If you like mashed potatoes snowy
white, peel them; if you like them with brown flecks, don't bother.
(One-third of the potato's nutrients are just beneath the skin.)
Do you like garlic? Add some when you mash the potatoes. Are
you a potatoes and gravy person? See the gravy recipe on page 158,
or skip the gravy and top a potato with grated cheese, sautéed vegetables, chopped cashews, or a handful of cooked corn or peas.*

2 potatoes, washed
2 to 3 tablespoons soy milk or nonfat dairy milk
Salt and pepper

1. Cut the potatoes into thirds. Place the potatoes in a
   saucepan and cover them with water. Bring the pot to a
   boil; reduce the heat, cover, and simmer until tender, about
   15 minutes.

2. Drain off the water. Mash the potatoes, mixing in the milk.
   Add more milk if the potatoes appear dry. Season with salt
   and pepper to taste.

NOTE: The water used for cooking the potatoes makes the beginning
of a great soup.

Makes one serving

Colcannon

PREPARATION TIME: 10 minutes

COOKING TIME: About 15 minutes

This food favorite from Ireland and Scotland has only two main in-gredients—potatoes and cabbage—and they're boiled together in one pot. It's a cheap, quick meal for a cold winter day.

2 medium russet or white potatoes, peeled
2 cups shredded green cabbage
1/2 cup chopped onion (about 1/2 medium)
1/4 cup soy milk or lowfat dairy milk
1 to 2 tablespoons grated Cheddar cheese or soy cheese
    (optional)
Salt and pepper

1. Cut the potatoes into 1-inch chunks. Place the potatoes in a medium pot, and cover them with water. Bring the water to a boil, and cook the potatoes until they are almost tender, about 10 minutes.

2. Add the cabbage and onion; continue cooking until the potatoes and cabbage are soft, about 5 minutes. Drain.

3. Add the milk and mash until the potatoes are smooth. Add cheese, if you desire. Taste; season with salt and pepper.

Makes two servings

Mashed Roots
with Horseradish

PREPARATION TIME: 5 minutes

COOKING TIME: About 20 minutes

If you've wondered what to do with a turnip, here's one answer.
They're also good sliced and eaten raw.

2 red or white potatoes, cut into eighths
1 turnip, peeled and cut into eighths
1 carrot, cut into eighths
1 large clove garlic
2 to 4 tablespoons soy milk or dairy milk
Salt and pepper
1 to 2 teaspoons horseradish
1 tablespoon minced fresh parsley (optional)

1. Place the potatoes, turnip, carrot, and garlic in a sauce-pan, and cover with water. Bring the water to a boil; reduce the heat. Put a lid on the pot, and simmer for about 20 minutes or until the vegetables are tender.
2. Drain the pot and add the milk. Mash and whip the mixture together until smooth. If necessary, add more milk. Season with salt and pepper. Taste, add horseradish, and stir. Serve sprinkled with parsley if you desire.

NOTE: Avoid brands of horseradish made with egg yolk.

Makes two servings

Scalloped Potatoes
Vegan-Style

PREPARATION TIME: 15 minutes

COOKING TIME: About 1 hour

This recipe tastes like old-fashioned scalloped potatoes, but without the milk and cheese. If you don't have a lid for your baking dish, cover it with foil.

1 teaspoon olive oil
1 white onion, finely chopped
4 cloves garlic, minced
1/4 cup tahini
2 tablespoons whole wheat flour
1/2 teaspoon salt
1 cup water
5 medium white or red potatoes

Preheat the oven to 400 degrees F.

1. Heat the oil in a skillet, and sauté the onion and garlic for 3 to 5 minutes on medium-high heat until the onion is soft and translucent.
2. In a blender or bowl, mix together the tahini, flour, salt, and water.

3. Thinly slice the potatoes. Don't bother to peel them. Arrange the potatoes in a lightly oiled 9-inch-square baking dish, overlapping them to cover the bottom of the dish. Spoon the onion and garlic mixture on top of the potato slices. Pour the tahini sauce over the top. Cover and bake for 1 hour. Uncover and bake another 5 to 10 minutes, until golden brown.

Makes two or three servings

Sweet Potato or Yam with Raisins and Pineapple

PREPARATION TIME: 6 minutes

COOKIING TIME: About 1 hour

Sweet potatoes are good enough to eat for dessert. The cooked texture of the light-skinned variety sweet potato will be dry and crumbly. The dark-skinned variety, sometimes labeled yam, is sweeter and more moist inside. Both are delicious.

1 sweet potato or yam
1 teaspoon raisins
1/8 teaspoon ground cinnamon
4 tablespoons canned unsweetened crushed pineapple,
    drained
1 tablespoon chopped walnuts

Preheat the oven to 375 degrees F.

1. Place potato on a baking sheet, and bake for 1 hour or until tender. Remove the potato from the oven and peel away the shell, or cut the potato in half and scoop out the inside.

2. Mash the potato with a fork in a small bowl. Add raisins, cinnamon, pineapple, and walnuts. If the potato mixture is dry, add pineapple liquid.

Makes two servings

CHAPTER 12

Desserts and Quick Breads

Here are sweet ideas for those times when you want to "boost your energy." If you're having a chocolate attack, Postmodern Chocolate Pudding is ready in 5 minutes, and Mountain High Chocolate Cake is made right in the baking pan so there's no mess to clean up. If you're not a chocoholic, there's plenty in this chapter for you, too.

Postmodern
Chocolate Pudding

PREPARATION TIME: 8 minutes

If you're not home alone, double the recipe and make someone happy. (If you double the recipe, microwave on High for 3 minutes, stir, and microwave on High for another 2 minutes.)

2 tablespoons sugar
2 tablespoons unsweetened baking cocoa powder
2 teaspoons firmly packed cornstarch
3/4 cup soy milk or dairy milk
1/4 teaspoon vanilla

1. In a 1-quart glass microwavable bowl, combine the sugar, cocoa, and cornstarch. Add 1/4 cup of the milk and stir until mixture is smooth and creamy. Add the remaining 1/2 cup milk and stir.

2. Stir once just before you close the microwave door because cornstarch quickly settles to the bottom of the bowl. Microwave the mixture for 1 1/2 minutes on High. Remove the bowl from the microwave; stir carefully (the mixture will be hot). Return the pudding to the microwave, and cook for another 1 1/2 minutes on High. The pudding will begin to thicken.

3. Remove the bowl from the microwave, and add the vanilla. Stir once. Let the pudding rest for 1 to 2 minutes. It will continue to thicken as it cools.

NOTE: Microwave cooking times can vary depending on the size of the cooking container, the power supply, and the temperature settings available on the oven. If you don't have a microwave, make the pudding in a small saucepan on top of the stove. Combine the ingredients in the pot. Cook over medium heat, stirring constantly, until the pudding comes to a boil. Lower the heat and gently simmer, stirring continuously until the pudding thickens, about 3 minutes. It is important to keep stirring to avoid burning or scorching.

Makes one serving

East Coast Custard

PREPARATION TIME: 12 minutes

COOKING TIME: About 1 1/2 hours

Stir up this recipe after dinner, and you'll have a marvelous late-night snack. It turns into smooth pudding as it cooks slowly in the oven. Serve it warm as is or topped with vanilla frozen yogurt.

1/2 teaspoon vegetable oil
2/3 cup cornmeal
1/4 teaspoon salt
1 teaspoon chopped fresh ginger or 1/2 teaspoon
    ground ginger
1/4 teaspoon nutmeg
2/3 cup raisins
4 cups soy milk or nonfat dairy milk
6 tablespoons maple syrup

Preheat the oven to 275 degrees F.

1. Lightly oil a 1 1/2- or 2-quart baking dish with vegetable oil. In a medium bowl, combine the cornmeal, salt, ginger, nutmeg, and raisins. Add 1 cup of the milk and the maple syrup. Stir to combine.

2. In a saucepan, heat 2 cups of milk to boiling. Gradually add the cornmeal mixture, stirring continuously. Reduce the heat to low and cook, stirring often, until the mixture is thick and smooth, about 10 minutes. Transfer to the prepared baking dish.

3. Pour the remaining 1 cup of milk on top of the cornmeal mixture. Bake until the milk is nearly all absorbed and the top of the pudding is golden brown. Begin checking for doneness in 1 hour. The baking time can vary 15 to 30 minutes depending on the coarseness of the cornmeal. It will be soft and creamy inside when done.

Makes six servings

Mountain-High
Chocolate Cake

PREPARATION TIME: 7 minutes

BAKING TIME: 25 to 30 minutes

The best thing about this recipe is what it doesn't have. It doesn't have eggs, milk, cholesterol, a mixing bowl to clean, or a pan to oil. It does deliver a delicious, dark chocolate cake. Serve the cake topped with a dollop of applesauce, and call it a rustic version of the famous German Sacher torte.

1 1/2 cups unbleached white flour
1/3 cup unsweetened baking cocoa powder
1 teaspoon baking soda
1/2 teaspoon salt
1 cup sugar
1 1/4 cups water
1/4 cup vegetable oil
2 teaspoons vanilla extract
2 tablespoons plain red or white vinegar

Preheat the oven to 375 degrees F.

1. Combine the flour, cocoa, baking soda, salt, and sugar in a glass, ceramic, or stainless steel baking pan (9-inch round, 8-inch square, or 9 × 6-inch rectangle).

2. In a small bowl, combine the water, oil, and vanilla. Pour the liquid into the dry ingredients, and whisk with a fork to

combine. Add the vinegar, and stir just until the vinegar is distributed around the batter. (There will be color variations in the batter from the reaction between the vinegar and baking soda.)

3. Bake for 25 to 30 minutes. Remove from the oven, and call your friends.

Makes six or eight servings

Vanilla Tapioca Pudding

PREPARATION TIME: 15 minutes

Eaten warm off the stove or chilled from the refrigerator, this creamy pudding will make you smile. Be bold and add fresh fruit, such as raspberries, strawberries, blueberries, bananas, mangos, pineapple, or orange slices.

3 tablespoons instant or minute tapioca
2 tablespoons sugar
2 cups soy milk or nonfat dairy milk
1/2 teaspoon vanilla extract

1. Combine the tapioca, sugar, and milk in a saucepan, and let it sit for 10 minutes to begin thickening.

2. On medium heat, bring the tapioca mixture to a boil, stirring constantly to prevent lumps and sticking. Lower heat; continue stirring, and cook for about 2 minutes.

3. Remove from heat, and stir in vanilla. Let it sit for 5 minutes before serving.

The pudding thickens as it cools.

Makes three servings

Warm Apple Slices

PREPARATION TIME: 3 minutes

COOKING TIME: 10 minutes

These plumped apples are delightful right out of the pot or spooned on top of hot oatmeal. If you're not in the mood for oatmeal, there's always ice cream.

1 apple
1 teaspoon butter
1/2 teaspoon maple syrup or sugar
1/4 teaspoon cinnamon

1. Quarter, core, and cut the apple into 1/8- to 1/4-inch slices.

2. In a medium pot, combine the apples with the other ingredients, cover, and simmer on medium-low heat for about 10 minutes.

Makes one or two servings

Chocolate Chip Cookies

If you're in a hurry, check out the nontraditional mixing option in this recipe.

1/2 cup butter, at room temperature
1 cup brown sugar or white sugar
1 egg
1 teaspoon vanilla
1/2 cup unbleached white all-purpose flour, plus
    2 tablespoons
1/2 cup whole wheat flour
1/2 teaspoon baking soda
1/2 teaspoon salt
1 cup chocolate chips
3/4 cup chopped walnuts (optional)

Preheat oven to 375 degrees.

Traditional Cookie Mixing
1. In a large bowl, cream together the butter and sugar until smooth. Beat in the egg and vanilla until well blended.
2. In a separate bowl, combine the white flour, whole wheat flour, baking soda, salt, chocolate chips, and nuts, if desired.
3. Stir the dry ingredients into the wet ingredients, mixing well.

4. Drop the batter by teaspoonfuls onto a greased cookie sheet about 2 inches apart. Bake 7 to 10 minutes until the bottoms are slightly browned. Check the oven after 7 minutes to avoid overbaking.

5. Remove the cookies with a spatula to a rack or dish to cool.

Nontraditional Cookie Mixing (It works!)
Dump everything into a large bowl and mush it together with your hands. Don't lick your fingers—raw batter with uncooked egg is a dangerous "treat" because of the risk of salmonella.

NOTE: Take the butter out of the refrigerator so that it can soften. If there's not time for that, put it in the microwave for a few seconds. It's much easier to cream butter when it's soft.

Makes about 2¹/₂ dozen, 2-inch cookies

Cinnamon Oatmeal Raisin Cookies

PREPARATION TIME: 15 minutes

COOKING TIME: 10 to 15 minutes per batch

If you think only chocolate will do, you'll change your mind when you taste these cinnamon oatmeal cookies.

1/2 cup butter (at room temperature)
3/4 cup brown sugar
1 large egg
1 teaspoon vanilla
11/4 cup rolled oats
1 cup whole wheat flour
1 teaspoon ground cinnamon
1/2 teaspoon baking powder
1/2 teaspoon baking soda
1/4 teaspoon salt
3/4 cup raisins

Preheat oven to 350 degrees F.

1. In a large bowl, cream together the butter and sugar until smooth. Add the egg and vanilla, and mix until well blended.

2. Add remaining ingredients, and mix until well combined.

3. Drop the dough in 1/4-cup mounds about 3 inches apart onto a lightly oiled baking sheet. Bake for 10 to 15 minutes, until golden. Check after 10 minutes to avoid overbaking. Use a spatula to transfer the cookies to a rack or plate to cool.

Makes 12 to 18 cookies

Baked Bananas

PREPARATION TIME: 3 minutes

COOKING TIME: 10 to 15 minutes

These bananas are sure to cause a conversation with the way they change color when they bake.

1 banana
1 to 2 tablespoons yogurt
1/8 teaspoon ground cinnamon

Preheat the oven to 400 degrees F.

1. Lay the unpeeled banana on a baking sheet. Make a slit along the length of the banana. Bake the banana with the slit side up for 10 to 15 minutes, or until the skin turns black.
2. Remove the banana from the oven and split open the peel. Top with a dollop of yogurt and a sprinkle of cinnamon, and eat it with a spoon.

Makes one serving

Blueberry Tart

Preparation Time: 6 minutes

Cooking Time: 30 minutes

Enjoy nibbling on this warm berry tart along with a hot cup of green tea.

2/3 cup whole wheat flour
1/2 cup sugar
11/2 teaspoons baking powder
1/4 teaspoon salt
2/3 cup soy milk or lowfat dairy milk
1/2 teaspoon vanilla
2 tablespoons butter, melted
2 cups blueberries

1. In a medium bowl, combine the flour, sugar, baking powder, and salt. Add the milk and vanilla, and stir until the batter is smooth.
2. Swirl the melted butter over the bottom of a 6 × 10-inch glass, ceramic, or stainless steel baking pan.
3. Pour in the batter, and sprinkle the top with the blueberries. Bake for 30 minutes or until the tart is golden brown.

NOTE: If you use frozen berries, thaw them first. If you use fresh berries, wash them and pick off any stems.

Makes four servings

Corn Bread Country-Style

PREPARATION TIME: 7 minutes

This tasty corn bread is an excellent accompaniment to a bowl of chili, soup, or salad.

1 cup cornmeal
1 cup whole wheat or white flour
$1/4$ cup brown or white sugar
2 teaspoons baking powder
$1/4$ teaspoon salt
1 cup soy milk or dairy milk
$1/4$ cup vegetable oil
1 egg

Preheat the oven to 425 degrees F.

1. Lightly oil a 9 × 6-inch baking dish or loaf pan with vegetable oil. In a large bowl, combine the cornmeal, flour, sugar, baking powder, and salt.

2. In a medium bowl, combine the milk, vegetable oil, and egg.

3. Pour the liquid mixture into the dry ingredients and stir just to combine. Do not overmix. Pour the mixture into the baking pan. Bake for 15 to 20 minutes until a knife inserted in the center comes out clean. Serve warm with honey or fruit preserves, if you desire.

NOTE: Corn flour or cornmeal, sometimes called polenta, work in this recipe. Depending on the type of cornmeal you use, you may need to add more liquid.

Makes six servings

Sunday Morning Muffins

PREPARATION TIME: 10 minutes

COOKING TIME: 18 to 20 minutes

Set out a jar of honey or jam, and enjoy these muffins straight from the oven. The trick to making high-rising, tender muffins is in the blending. Too much stirring makes them tough. When you combine the flour mixture with the applesauce mixture, stir only until the dry ingredients become moist. If a few lumps remain, that's okay.

1 cup whole wheat flour
1 cup white flour
1/4 cup sugar
2 teaspoons baking powder
3/4 teaspoon baking soda
1/2 teaspoon ground cinnamon
3/4 cup raisins
2 cups unsweetened applesauce
1/4 cup vegetable oil

Preheat the oven to 375 degrees F.

1. In a large bowl, add the flours, sugar, baking powder, baking soda, cinnamon, and raisins. Stir to combine.

2. In a medium bowl, whisk the applesauce and oil together.

3. Add the applesauce mixture to the flour mixture, stirring just to moisten. Spoon the batter into a lightly oiled standard muffin tin. Bake for 18 to 20 minutes or until golden.

Makes 12 muffins

CHAPTER 13

Drinks

Be Fluid

Whether you choose bottled water from the supermarket or a glass of cold tap water with a slice of lemon, you'll be surprised by how much water you'll naturally drink when it's near at hand. Drink plenty of water, and also enjoy the recipes in this chapter for coffee, tea, and blender quenchers.

Take a Coffee Break

If coffee has become an integral part of your life during long nights of studying, here are some ideas to help you use it to your best advantage. Caffeine is similar to amphetamines but milder in its effects. It is a central nervous system stimulant that makes you feel more alert, temporarily relieves fatigue, and promotes quick thinking. It doesn't take much caffeine to accomplish this feeling of well-being. The amount in one or two ordinary cups of coffee is enough. However, at greater doses (five to six cups or more), caffeine can produce negative effects such as nervousness, anxiety, and panic attacks. Although coffee isn't a health food, recent research has turned up very little scientific evidence to indict a moderate intake of two cups daily.

Prepared coffee doesn't keep well. Warming it over a burner for only about 20 minutes can make the taste bitter. If you are making coffee for one person, the filter method is a good choice. It's simple to make only one or two cups at a time, and cleanup is easy. Measure 2 rounded tablespoons of ground coffee per cup into a filter-lined cone poised over your pot or cup. (In the world of coffee, a cup is 6 ounces, not the 8 ounces in a standard measuring cup. So if you are using a full measuring cup or a giant coffee mug to measure water, your coffee will probably be weak.) Rinse the pot and cup with hot water before you make the coffee, and the drink will remain hot longer. Heat cold fresh water just until it boils. Remove the water from the heat. Next, add just a few splashes of water to the coffee grounds to moisten them slightly. Let them absorb the water before pouring on the rest. This will prevent the water from going through the grounds too quickly without extracting maximum flavor.

Coffee Brazil

PREPARATION TIME: 5 minutes

This fragrant cup of coffee is a quick pick-me-up.

1 cup coffee
1 sliver lemon peel

Pour hot coffee into a cup. Twist the lemon peel to release its oils. Rub the yellow side of the peel around the rim of the cup for a citrus-flavored coffee.

Makes one serving

Café au Lait

PREPARATION TIME: 7minutes

This foamy mixture satisfies first thing in the morning or late at night. You will need a blender to foam the milk. It won't reach the heights of the steamed milk from an espresso bar, but it won't cost as much, either.

1/2 cup soy milk or dairy milk
1 teaspoon honey
1/2 cup freshly brewed strong coffee

Heat the milk and honey to a boil, and then whip it in a blender for 30 seconds. Next, pour the coffee into a cup and add the milk mixture.

Makes one serving

Coffee Alaska

PREPARATION TIME: 5 minutes

Here is the perfect drink for anytime you feel the impulse for something sweet.

1 cup freshly brewed coffee
1/4 cup soy ice cream, nonfat frozen yogurt, or dairy ice cream

Pour the hot coffee over vanilla or chocolate ice cream or frozen yogurt. If you drink the coffee quickly enough—before all the ice cream melts—you'll have a delicious warm puddle to sip from the bottom of your cup.

Makes one serving

Banana Express

PREPARATION TIME: 5 minutes

Here is a great way to use an over-ripe banana and whip up a cool coffee treat.

1/2 cup strong coffee
1/4 cup soy milk
1/2 ripe banana, peeled and sliced
1 ice cube

Whip the ingredients in a blender until smooth; while the blender is turning, add the ice cube through the small opening in the blender lid, and blend on high for about 30 seconds. Pour into a glass. Enjoy!

Makes one serving

Mocha Coffee

PREPARATION TIME: 5 minutes

Make this delicious coffee with equal parts coffee and hot chocolate.

1/2 cup coffee
1/2 cup hot chocolate
Grated orange peel

Stir the hot coffee and hot chocolate together. Serve topped with grated orange peel.

Makes one serving

The Tea Zone

All tea varieties come from the same plant, *Camellia sinensis*. After they are harvested, different processing methods turn them into one of three basic types of tea: black, green, and oolong. Herbal "teas" do not come from the tea plant but are blends of other plant leaves, flowers, roots, and spices. Tea has about half the caffeine as a comparable cup of coffee. Make tea with fresh water; water that has been kept warm for a period of time will make flat-tasting tea. Rinse your cup with hot water before making tea so that the brew will stay warm longer. Allow the tea to steep 3 to 5 minutes to extract flavor and color. Serve immediately. Tea doesn't hold up well.

Chocolate Chai

Preparation Time: 7 minutes

When you feel the impulse for something chocolate, make this simple duet.

1 cup hot water
1 commercial chai tea bag (without sugar)
$1/3$ cup dairy milk or soy milk
2 teaspoons cocoa
2 teaspoons sugar or honey

1. Pour hot water directly over tea bag in a preheated oversized mug.
2. While the tea steeps (3 to 5 minutes), heat milk, cocoa, and sugar in small saucepan, stirring to dissolve cocoa.
3. Remove tea bag. Pour the hot milk mixture into tea. Taste. If you like sweeter chai, add more sugar.

Makes one serving

Hot Apple Tea

PREPARATION TIME: 6 minutes

Relax with this warm, fragrant brew. Try Berry Zinger, Peppermint, Lemon Spice, or your favorite herbal tea.

1 cup apple juice
1 herbal tea bag

Bring apple juice to a boil in a small saucepan. Remove from heat and add tea bag. Steep for 5 minutes. Pour into a warmed mug.

NOTE: If the tea you choose is full of strong, sharp flavor like Berry Zinger, use half apple juice and half water.

Makes one serving

Blender Quenchers

Smoothies are a speedy way to give yourself a refreshing lift. They can be a fast meal or a relaxing drink for sipping. Inventing smoothies is simple. Ripe fruits blended with juices, yogurt, or milk and sweetened with honey or maple syrup make the base. Add a dash of vanilla, cinnamon, or nutmeg and you're ready to go. (Use ripe fruit, and you may not need to add sweetener.) If you want a savory veggie drink, try Pink Tomato Swirl (page 244).

When you're in the mood for a "chiller" drink and plan to add ice, crushed ice is the easiest to use. If you add ice cubes, make sure the blender is whizzing around at top speed, and that you add one cube at a time. Sweeten your drink before you chill it. Honey, for example, doesn't want to loosen up and mix once it's chilled. Ice dilutes the flavor of a drink, so taste-test as you go. You can also add sparkling water; add it after the drink is blended, because you'll lose the fizz if it's whirled in a blender. Enjoy!

Tofu Berry Shake

PREPARATION TIME: 4 minutes

This is an amazingly luxurious shake. You will never recognize tofu in this form. Honest, this is sooooo delicious.

1 (6-ounce) can pineapple juice
1 ripe banana
1/2 cup silken tofu (4 ounces)
1/2 to 1 cup fresh or frozen strawberries
1/2 teaspoon vanilla
1 to 2 tablespoons sugar or maple syrup (optional)

Combine all ingredients except the sugar in a blender and puree until smooth. Taste. Add sugar or maple syrup if you desire.

Makes two servings

Yogurt Fruit Shake

PREPARATION TIME: 4 minutes

Got a blender? Here's a fast way to start the day.

3/4 cup plain nonfat yogurt
1 cup chopped fruit (pear, pineapple, berries, banana—
    the riper the better)
1/2 teaspoon vanilla
1 teaspoon honey, sugar, or maple syrup (optional)

Place ingredients in blender, and process until smooth.

Makes two servings

Pink Tomato Swirl

If you like gazpacho, you will love this creamy tomato drink.

1/4 cup plain yogurt
1 cup tomato juice
1 clove garlic, chopped
1/4 cup peeled, chopped cucumber
1 teaspoon seeded, chopped jalapeño chile
Tabasco (optional)

Combine the ingredients in a blender. Add a dash of Tabasco, if you desire.

Makes one serving

CHAPTER 14

Beer and Vegetarianism

Jeff Byles

Beer and college are closely, and often notoriously, paired in popular imagination.

Movies like *Animal House* and *Revenge of the Nerds* stereotype college beer drinkers as brew-guzzling, hard-partying maniacs. Strange collegiate traditions routinely involve emptying beer kegs. Scenes of brew-induced mayhem around campus are, unfortunately, all too common in the real world. Beer's reputation has accordingly suffered.

The recent renaissance in microbrewing shows that beer has a tradition all its own. Microbrewers have revived centuries-old brewing traditions, making their beer in small batches with care and pride. A few years ago there were just a few brands of beer; today there are literally hundreds.

"Craft-brewed" beer has restored the dignity, quality, and pleasure to a pint of frothy ale or lager. Starting with fresh malted barley, seasoning the brew with extravagantly floral hop flowers, and fermenting with authentic yeast strains, craft brewers prize their ingredients much as vegetarians might prize a perfectly ripe avocado.

Actually, beer and vegetarianism have a lot in common. When people encounter a vegetarian, they often ask incredulously, "But what do you eat?" It is as if the world of food without meat amounted to a few heads of wilted iceberg lettuce and a pitiable stalk of broccoli. As any vegetarian knows, a little patient experimentation yields delicious meat-free rewards. What plump roast could ever compare with a tangy, succulent dish of pad thai?

Similarly, many beer consumers find it hard to believe that there is a vast world of beer beyond the pale-hued, mass-produced beers like Budweiser, Coors, and Miller. While those beers are not necessarily bad, drinking a mass-market "light" beer is like eating packaged macaroni and cheese when you could just as easily be dining on an elegant dish of Pasta al Pesto.

Like vegetarian cuisine, the world of beer is bursting with flavor. Try whatever comes your way: a nicely balanced pale ale, crisp with hops; a dark and roasty stout, thick and velvety as a milkshake; or real Belgian ale, tart and sweet with a delicately soft maltiness.

Besides increasing your gustatory pleasure, exploring beer is a way of educating your palate—much like exploring the unfamiliar territory of painting is how one learns to appreciate art.

This is not to say that there aren't other, more practical uses for beer. There are a variety of resourceful ways the steepings of malts can improve human morale. Should you find yourself in the possession of a quantity of beer that is, for whatever reasons, undrinkable, do not despair.

According to naturopaths, beer makes a wonderful shampoo, hydrating the hair while adding protein from the grains. Many home brewers claim that beer serves tolerably well as an insect barrier, and they dispense it liberally around their garden. Some other, perhaps unorthodox, uses for our wonderfully versatile malt beverage are as follows:

- Keep it in a sacred vessel and use sparingly for rituals honoring Ninkasi, the goddess of brewing.
- Freeze it for use in "beer-sicles."
- Age it carefully for a few months in a sealed container to make malt vinegar.
- Boil off most of the liquid to obtain "essence of beer," creating a captivating new perfume and cologne.

When William Blake wrote that the road of excess leads to the palace of wisdom, I do not believe he was talking about beer. Should you happen to venture that way, however, there are a few things to know about how beer affects the body. While cures for hangovers are prolific, beware: they are mostly the stuff of myth.

The liver needs only two essential aids to process the alcohol in beer—plenty of time and water. Because alcohol is a strong diuretic, it causes the body to lose water. Therefore, drinking water before and while you drink alcohol will help avoid that morning headache. Food also slows the rate of alcohol absorption from the stomach, so having a plate of falafel with a pitcher of ale will help ease the effects of alcohol on the body.

Researchers have found that women need to be particularly careful when drinking, because women's alcohol tolerance varies at different times of the month. A premenstrual woman will be most vulnerable to alcohol, because during this time enzyme action in the liver slows, causing more alcohol to accumulate in the bloodstream.

Beer can indeed be a profound part of anyone's education. Rich in tradition, robust in culture, and mellifluous in taste, beer offers a wealth of meaning unlike any other beverage. That luminous pint of ale can incite the intellect and soothe the soul.

Now that's beer for thought.

Resources

Good Books

Klein, Naomi. *No Logo: Taking Aim at the Brand Bullies.* New York: Picador, 2002.

Robbins, John. *Diet for a New America.* Walpole, NM: Stillpoint, 1987.

Schlosser, Eric. *Fast Food Nation: The Dark Side of the All-American Meal.* New York: HarperCollins, 2002

Good Group

EarthSave International
1509 Seabright Avenue, Suite B1
Santa Cruz, CA 95062
Phone: (800) 362-3648
Web site: www.earthsave.org

EarthSave International promotes the benefits of plant-based food choices for our health, our environment, and a more compassionate world. Contact them for information on volunteer opportunities, educational materials, or questions about Earth-Save's new projects.

Good Web Sites

Farm Animal Reform Movement
www.farmusa.org

Farm Sanctuary
www.farmsanctuary.org

Greenpeace
www.greenpeace.org

National Coalition Against the Misuse of Pesticides
www.beyondpesticides.org

North American Vegetarian Society
www.navs-online.org

Oxfam America
www.oxfamamerica.org

People for the Ethical Treatment of Animals (PETA)
www.peta.com

Tufts University Nutrition Navigator
www.navigator.tufts.edu

Vegan Action
www.vegan.org

Veggies Unite
www.vegweb.com

VegSource
www.vegsource.com

Youth for Environmental Sanity (YES)
www.yesworld.org

Index